Women Survivors of Violence

Women Survivors of Violence

Genesis and Growth of a State Support System

Anjali Dave

TISS
Tata Institute of Social Sciences

Orient BlackSwan

WOMEN SURVIVORS OF VIOLENCE

ORIENT BLACKSWAN PRIVATE LIMITED

Registered Office
3-6-752 Himayatnagar, Hyderabad 500 029 (Telangana), INDIA
e-mail: centraloffice@orientblackswan.com

Other Offices
Bangalore, Bhopal, Bhubaneshwar, Chennai,
Ernakulam, Guwahati, Hyderabad, Jaipur, Kolkata,
Lucknow, Mumbai, New Delhi, Noida, Patna

First published by Orient Blackswan Pvt. Ltd. 2015

ISBN 978-81-250-5915-8

Typeset in
Minion Pro 11/13.2
by PrePSol Enterprises Pvt. Ltd, Haryana

Printed in India at
Glorious Printers, Delhi

Published by
Orient Blackswan Private Limited
1/24 Asaf Ali Road
New Delhi 110 002
e-mail: delhi@orientblackswan.com

Contents

Tables

Figures

Abbreviations

ACS	Additional Chief Secretary
BSW	Bachelor in Social Work
CAWC	Crime against Women Cell
CP	Commissioner of Police
CrPC	Criminal Procedure Code
CRVAW	Centre for Research on Violence against Women
CSWB	Central Social Welfare Board
DCP	Deputy Commissioner of Police
DGP	Director-General of Police
DIG (PAW)	Deputy Inspector General of Police (Prevention of Atrocities on Women)
DWCD	Department of Women and Child Development
FAP	Field Action Project
GR	Government Resolution
IAS	Indian Administrative Service
IASSW	International Association of Schools of Social Work
IAWS	Indian Association of Women's Studies
ICRW	International Centre for Research on Women
IG	Inspector General
IPC	Indian Penal Code
IPS	Indian Police Service
MDS	Mahila Dakshata Samiti
MoU	Memorandum of Understanding
NCW	National Commission for Women
NGO	Non-governmental Organisation
SMEG	Strategic Management Exercise Group
SP	Superintendent of Police
TISS	Tata Institute of Social Sciences
UNDP	United Nations Development Programme
UNFPA	United Nations Population Fund
UNIFEM	United Nations Development Fund for Women
USAID	United States Agency for International Development
WAF	Welfare Agencies Fund
WCSW	Women-Centred Social Work

FOREWORD

It has been a great pleasure to read the fascinating journey of Anjali Dave from childhood to professional maturity, and how she developed a feminist outlook and a strong commitment to social work intervention in the area of domestic violence against women as the main target of her work. Her highly focused approach, which enabled her to stay with the issue rather than take on all aspects of violence against women, has been the single reason for the success achieved in the task she set out to undertake. The late Professor Meenakshi Apte's vision, based on grassroots realities and an innovative approach to problem-solving, set her on the course of working with the police on the issue. As she stated, the Special Cell, set up in the Office of the Commissioner of Police, 'developed into socio-legal work—a combination of social analysis and social work interventions, informed by a feminist analysis of society, women and the law'.

The study is based on her personal journey through several ups and downs, struggles in a setting where professional social work intervention was little understood, and professional social workers seen as outsiders and charged with expressions of emotion in moments of elation or frustration, as each step involved tremendous inputs to move the work forward. Her book has a very human approach, combined with incisive analysis and an objective view of the dynamics at each stage of crisis or achievement. This is what makes it exceptionally readable.

I have known Anjali Dave since her days as an undergraduate student—when I was at the College of Social Work, affiliated to Mumbai University (at Nirmala Niketan), as Vice Principal and Principal—and again as my student, and later colleague, at the Tata Institute of Social Sciences, where I was Director. This has given me a great opportunity to know her as a person, and the intensity and depth that she brings to her work. Her output in the work of the Special Cells bears testimony to it.

The women who came to seek help, she observes, wanted the violence to cease in the main, and were not looking for court action, criminal or civil. 'They needed assistance to challenge violence (physical and/or emotional) and help them rebuild their sense of self and dignity, while regaining the ability to earn and provide for themselves and their families.' They wanted the abuse to stop and not to end their marriages, and 'actively resisted going to court, seeing it only as the last step if the relationships did not work out'—which the Special Cell saw as remedial action, rather than preventive. On the other hand, as elaborated in the book, the issue of intra-familial assaults and interpersonal conflicts are not seen as crimes by the police. 'Their perceptions are influenced by deeply entrenched beliefs about the sanctity of the family, the superiority of the male, and the forbearance of women—the family as a unit has to be preserved at all costs.' Basically, both women and men are brought up with the beliefs of a patriarchal social structure, which legitimises male authority over female; and, therefore, power and control vests in the male.

While this is the societal perspective that results in the attitude of male superiority, the social workers of the Special Cell brought in an attitude of respect for the woman's dignity and self-worth, enabling her to decide for herself the change she desired in her situation, and assisting her in achieving it through her written application, the interview process of reflection, and through empowering her capacity to make her own decisions concerning what she wanted for herself, her relationship with her spouse, and her marriage. Thus, the balance of power is sought to be shifted to arrive at the solution the woman views as one she can live with in a non-violent environment. In the process, social workers also reach out to the husband to confront him with his behaviour and examine alternatives with his spouse, which can lead to a mutual agreement. It is obvious that the Special Cell provides a nurturing and supportive environment that allows emotionally charged women to express themselves, keeping as its reference framework the fact that the workers were in a legal setting.

From the above, it can be seen that the work of the social workers centres round the prevention of violence, counselling of both the woman seeking help and her spouse, and those in her relationship network. It also entailed legal and police intervention with police perceptions being varied, depending on their individual personal beliefs. In most cases, the higher the position, the greater the support for the work; at the middle level, there were those who supported the work, and those who questioned the presence of persons outside the police system, who were granted physical access—in the form of premises, equipment and administrative support—and access to the women who come to the police station for help with their abusive husbands. Gender also played a role as female workers, even trainers, faced more problems, while there was greater bonding among the male staff of the Special Cells. Women police also face similar gender discrimination, as problems of equality, prejudice and limited opportunities prevail in a dominant male environment as the police system. The system is seen more as male than as female in its structure and in the type of mandate it carries for law and order and crime, which is given greater emphasis in the system than the implementation of social legislation.

It further points to a greater reason in favour of a multidisciplinary approach to implementing social legislation by introducing partnerships, such as the one with social workers in the Special Cells, especially for work on a wide spectrum of issues concerning women and children in a country as vast and highly populated as ours. In terms of physical topography, India has plains, forests, mountains, and rivers that isolate some of its citizens, large, unmanageable metropolises, and smaller, more manageable towns and villages that are poorly connected to the main thoroughfares. It also has a population of over a billion, which is more diverse than in any other country. In such a context, no one profession can hope to impact the country's problems, and a multidisciplinary approach becomes the most suitable method in problem-solving.

Public-private partnership, which is essentially multidisciplinary, could go a long way in the implementation of all social legislation; however, its purpose is often little understood in the entrenched systems of the police or the bureaucracy. Used to control mechanisms that spring from their power status, it is difficult for them to envisage a partnership. The experience has been similar with regard to a professional partnership with the national bureaucracy in the area of child protection. While the State has both legal and social responsibility for problems of all kinds with respect to violence against women, the nature of the problem requires more professional social case work and counselling intervention than criminal or legal redress. Such programmes require a type of funding that only the State can provide—from our taxes, paid from our hard-earned money—hence, it has a responsibility to meet the requirements of its citizens, whether it is infrastructure development or programmes for vulnerable groups. A partnership is beneficial to both—the intervention in a police setting gives it legitimacy on behalf of the women seeking help, and at the same time, provides the police assistance with cases beyond their policing skills.

However, the many problems faced by the Special Cells in the process of institutionalising this partnership were horrendous; they faced several disappointments till the partnership was sealed in Mumbai with the police accepting the Special Cells as a part of its service, and the Government of Maharashtra, Department of Women and Child Development, taking financial responsibility. This development has led to several other states setting up such Cells, some through bilateral and multilateral donors, thus upscaling an initiative started as a field action project to a recognised service for women in abusive relationships, who face physical injuries and emotional pain, and the loss of dignity and self-worth.

The importance of this achievement through three decades of consistent action and perseverance to achieve its goals, is a demonstration of the need for such 'laboratory' projects in institutions of social work education. These are start-ups, generally supported by donor organisations and corporates, to demonstrate a new thrust or strategy or a new model of organising service delivery, nurtured in the social work educational institution through its faculty and students teams. As the arena of professional social work has demonstrated, such start-ups are often taken over by national, state, or local governments. Innovation is not confined to the technical field or to the Indian Institutes of Technology. These have also been demonstrated in the social sector by institutions for professional social work education, as much as by other social activists. Unlike technological innovations, the agency taking over for replication and upscaling is not a commercial organisation, but the government.

As an educational institution, Tata Institute of Social Sciences has not only developed a service in a legal setting, but has also developed training programmes for social workers to update their skills, and for allied systems like the police and the judiciary. It has also undertaken research to identify the gaps in service, which has further added to the quality of the work undertaken, and also on other areas related to the problem of domestic violence. The latter research efforts ultimately led to the establishment of the Centre for Research on Violence Against Women. Hence, the action programme becomes a base for training/classroom teaching and research in an academic environment. Anjali Dave's work also demonstrates an abiding belief in the basic principles of professional social work—upholding people's dignity and self-worth; providing an opportunity for self-determination, that is, exploring what a person seeking help wants and is prepared to do; the latent capacity, to be nurtured, of people to develop the ability to take their life situations into their own hands; and a belief in the equality of caste, class, gender, age, and religion.

A well-documented professional treatise, this book is also an interesting and very readable account of a process in which the author's emotional and professional involvement are transparent, making it a very humanistic approach to recording an entire journey.

Mumbai,
18 April 2015

Armaity S. Desai,
former Chairperson, University Grants Commission, New Delhi;
former Director, Tata Institute of Social Sciences, Mumbai

Acknowledgements

This book tells the story of women's struggle to live lives of dignity and self-respect, and marks women's courage to struggle against violence in our lives.

I am grateful to several people and institutions. My thanks to the Bombay Police and the Maharashtra police system, which opened their doors to build a strategic alliance to address Violence against Women, and for undertaking the long journey to make the Special Cells a support system of the State.

Thanks to the Special Cells Team for upholding our shared vision of rebuilding and strengthening violated women to be safe strong and secure.

To my friends, who all contributed to our growing understanding of the subject 'Woman'. To friends in the women's movement for holding up the critical lens, and in the state system for joining hands on the issue of Violence against Women.

To Dr S. Parasuraman (Director, TISS), for cajoling me to put pen to paper and produce this record/publication and Dr Surinder Jaswal (former Dean, School of Social Work) for convincing me of the significance of writing of a field action project in Social Work education.

And to all those who literally saw me through the writing period:

a) The TISS–London School of Economics and Political Science Fellowship;
b) TISS–SS–and the Centre for Equity for Women, Children and Families, for giving me sabbatical leave;
c) For ploughing through the first draft, Sangeeta Chatterji, C. Rammanohar Reddy, and Nandita Gandhi;
d) Anil Menon, for painstakingly editing and readying the manuscript;
e) Proteeti Banerjee at Orient BlackSwan for the final editing;
f) Durgesh Solanki, for helping me with the literature review; and
g) Savitri Jagtap, for typing my handwritten work.

I am grateful to my teachers for reposing faith in my work, to Professor Meenakshi Apte in social work, and Mr J. F. Ribeiro in the Police System.

I gratefully acknowledge Dr Armaity S. Desai for writing the Foreword.

And finally, to my grandparents, parents, family, and Venkat for their 'unconditional love.'

1

Evolution of Thought on Violence Against Women

The Context

Location—physical, ideological, temporal—seems a good starting point to explain the work of the Special Cell and my involvement with it. I came to the Tata Institute of Social Sciences (TISS) in Mumbai in 1980 after a Bachelor's degree in social work (BSW), and a year of fieldwork that introduced me to the concepts of political education, conscientisation, and the critical thinking of Brazilian educator Paulo Freire. My grandparents' stories of the independence movement and their active participation in community building for a new modern nation were part of my context. My grandparents were Gandhian, and this perspective coloured my day-to-day meanings. This included a belief in democracy, an awareness of the ills of casteism, a reluctance to practise its rites and rituals, a conviction that men and women were equal, and an understanding that one had to be respectful to all.

From the early 1960s, I remember the morning ritual of tea, and radio and newspaper headlines. My grandparents and my grand-aunt discussed political happenings in the country, along with voicing opinions shaped by their reading and what they had heard. I recall the names of the magazines and booklets that came into the household—*Samarpan, Khadi Patrika,* and so on—and have the distinct memory that none of them had pictures for me to make sense of the articles. (For I could not read Gujarati very well.)

I marvel at our minds and the way they absorb from the environment. This infusion from family beliefs kept me buoyant in my early days at the Special Cell. I associated the problems that came to the Special Cell with my childhood memories and experiences, particularly how issues were viewed by my grandmother, grandaunt and mother. My first lessons in feminism were learnt from them. I understood a lot of what I heard, read and discussed later because the foundation had been laid in political discussions at home. My grandparents accepted that theirs had been a child marriage, narrating stories of how young wives went to their in-laws during the day, worked in the household, and returned to their parents before nightfall—the walk to and fro, carrying their *potlas* (bags), and the laughter. My grandaunt had returned to the home a widowed young mother, and her brothers looked after her family, treating their sister as 'auspicious'. My grandmother and grandaunt had been educated till the fifth or seventh grade, but my mother and her sister were graduates. So my family had a liberal bent of mind, and they wanted me to equip myself to earn and stand on my own feet.

Were they Marxist or socialist? Looking back, I feel no label fully captures who they were, and that there were even strands of radical and post-modernist thinking in them. There are innumerable stories to tell, each deserving its own interpretation. They were all a part of my growing up, became a part of me, and helped me understand and relate to other women's lives as well as my own.

Later, fieldwork introduced me to social problems such as wife beating, alcoholism, poverty, and the lack of education, awareness, and basic amenities, all largely within a class context—rich and poor. Simply put, this was understood as the rich being bad people and the poor being good. I came alive to nuanced socio-political realities only when I consciously worked with abused women and tackled the issue of violence against women. At a theoretical level, patriarchy is the reason most commonly cited for violence against women in society. Patriarchy is defined as a system of dominance legitimated within the family and society, according males superior rights, privileges, authority, and power. Although violence against women is nothing new, its conceptualisation and recognition gained with the second-wave feminism.

The concept of patriarchy has been useful in explaining the depth, pervasiveness, and interconnectedness of different aspects of women's subordination. It has also provided a means to account for the different forms of gender inequality over time, class, and ethnic groups (Walby 1990). During my graduate days, the term evoked images of class hierarchies, gender hierarchies, and dominance and power. But arrangements in the family, community and social system that reinforce domination became clearer during the Special Cell years. The concept was also useful in that it directed the gaze towards social contexts, rather than towards overbearing individual males who had been conditioned to dominate.

My vivid memories of the work with women relate to sociologist Sylvia Walby's six different structures of patriarchy—the patriarchal mode of production, patriarchal relations in paid work, patriarchal relations in the state, male violence, patriarchal relations in sexuality, and patriarchal relations in cultural institutions. Patriarchal systems at the macro level (bureaucracies, government, law, market, religion) are buttressed by patriarchal relations at the micro level (interactions, families, organisations, patterned behaviour between intimates). At a more abstract level, patriarchy exists as a system of social relations that varies across time and space. Gender hierarchy is the defining feature of a patriarchal system—age, race, class, sexuality, religion, historical location, and nationality mediate gender statuses, assigning males and females varying amounts of social value, privilege and power, all apportioned to control women.

Attending an Indian Association of Women's Studies (IAWS) conference in Kerala in April 1984 introduced me to the world of women's studies and feminism. But it was a paper on patriarchy and the law, presented by Upendra Baxi at the conference, that opened my eyes to social structures beyond women, and made the interconnections clearer. Participating in different programmes and campaigns of the women's movement familiarised me with a wide variety of isms, waves, and schools of thoughts. It is through these that I grew to understand the four main strands of feminism—the liberal, the Marxist, the socialist Marxist, and the radical. I became acquainted with the names and ideas of Simone de Beauvoir, Betty Friedman and Shulamith Firestone.

Radical feminist thought sees sexual practice as socially constructed around male, not female, notions of desire. Sexuality is a major site of male domination over women, through which men impose their notion of femininity on women. The realisation that male violence against women is part of a system of controlling women was gradually seeping into the consciousness of Indian women's movements at the time. I gradually began to comprehend the close connection between caste, class and the state, which together function as the structural framework of the institutions of family, community and tribe, within which gender relations operate. And the control of women's sexuality was of prime importance to maintaining the caste structure.

The women's movement in India re-taught me history and geography. It made me aware of the 'modern women project' (Chatterjee 1993: Chs. 6, 7), that women's bodies were the focus of violence during the partition of India, and the role the Constitution, Five-Year Plans, policies, and programmes have played in the construction of the idea of Indian women. A feminist consciousness and critique emerged in multiple mass movements in the 1960s and 1970s, in which both men and women participated. In these struggles, women created a 'space' for themselves, even though men were present as participants and as leaders in the movements. From the late 1970s, separate women's cells to address gender concerns emerged in these mass movements, which played a critical role in the evolution of a feminist consciousness. The United Nations declared 1975 as the international year of women, and the Government of India appointed a committee to undertake a comprehensive examination of all issues related to the rights and status of women in the country, in the context of changing social and economic conditions.

My participation in the meetings and workshops now considered historic milestones began in the 1980s. Women's groups across the country had begun to strive hard to get laws implemented through protests, demanding that the police, lawyers and judges be sensitised, and popularising the legal changes through literacy programmes. Several reports on the implementation of these laws in the 1980s pointed to lacunae at various levels, especially the poor rates of registration and conviction, and a legal system enmeshed in stereotypical notions of 'victim' women. After about a decade of work, it became evident in the first half of the 1990s that the process of actualisation of women's rights as citizens would be a difficult one. In the police stations or in the courts, women's rights were predominantly being interpreted in terms of their identities as wives, sisters, or mothers. Moreover, the terrain of criminal law held out very little for women's complex needs in the family.

Violence against women includes any form of coercion, power, or control exerted on a woman by her intimate partner or his extended kin. This involves physical, sexual, verbal, and mental abuse, sex-selective foeticide, female infanticide, and discrimination. With the emergence of an autonomous women's movement, the issues raised by feminists centred on violence against women, which included domestic violence, crimes against women, sexual harassment, rape, dowry deaths, wife battering, and reproductive health issues such as foeticide, invasive technologies, and harmful contraceptives. Through campaigns on these issues, the Indian women's movement exposed patriarchal values that legitimised chastity and sexual 'purity', relating a woman's 'honour' and body to her social identity. The other side of this was stigmatising a 'dishonoured' woman.

The household was opened up to show it as a unit of exploitation that controlled women's freedom and choice. Two important campaigns in this connection were the ones against rape in the mid-1970s (the Mathura rape case in 1972 and the Rameeza Bee case in 1978), and against dowry deaths in the early 1980s. These campaigns are important to understand how the women's movement raised the issue of violence against women by theorising on cruelty in the public and private spheres.

The other issue that became important was dowry deaths. In the campaign against dowry deaths, feminists interrogated the nature of the 'private sphere' and challenged the received binary of public and private. The campaign focused on the violence inflicted on women to obtain dowries—in the form of murder and by pushing victims into committing suicide. Feminists joined forces with neighbourhood groups, trade unions, and teachers' associations to strengthen the campaign against dowry. Emerging feminist groups initiated new approaches to enhance public awareness of the dowry problem, such as street plays and pledge-taking ceremonies against the practice.

Introspection on the movements' successes and failures led to the establishment of women's centres of two kinds. One provided a mixture of legal aid, healthcare and counselling. In these centres, individual cases concerning legal and health problems were dealt with. The other concentrated on providing services to individual women from a feminist perspective, helping them realise their rights. What made these distinct from earlier women's centres was their feminist approach to issues. These centres used the notion of 'gendered rights' to challenge the welfare approach of earlier women's groups.

Women's groups and activists demanded that the police and courts take cognisance of violence against women in marriages and families. The expectation was that the police would recognise such incidents as crimes and respond to them, not view them as private happenings within households, where they had no role to play. However, in the course of their campaigns, it was discovered that the law does not only reflect patriarchal relations, but also reproduces patriarchal relations in the family, the community, and the state. Thus, the law is in a position to regulate and limit women's options and choices, and reforms to it had to be seen as a practical gender need. Against this background, the Special Cell, with a feminist perspective that provided socio-legal aid to survivors of violence, came to be seen as a strategic interest (Kabeer 1995).

This was the backdrop against which the Project for Women in Distress was envisaged by Professor M. J. Apte, head of the Department of Family and Child Welfare at TISS. Her experience in the field, innovative ideas and convictions led to the project being initiated in July 1984. Professor Apte, who was my teacher and fieldwork supervisor, continually drew me into discussions on contemporary issues, as well as activities beyond the job in the department. I thus took part in formulating and writing the project proposal, as well as in the initial meetings that led to setting up the project.

Genesis of this Book

In 2009, the Special Cell project completed 25 years. I wrote a note to the director of TISS, S. Parasuraman, about our plans to mark the occasion, and asked for his suggestions. A reply came, outlining the papers that could be written on our interventions to prevent violence against women. I had also asked for some distance from the work on violence against women, but he cajoled me into a project of penning down an account of the Special Cell's journey through the past quarter of a century.

Different people gave me different reasons why I should undertake this work. To get a PhD topped the list, while others mentioned recording the Indian experience of dealing with violence against women, and working in the criminal justice system. What finally convinced me was the fact that I was a faculty member at TISS, the academic institution that had initiated the Special Cell as a field action project (FAP), and supported it through thick and thin. Field action projects are meant to promote innovation and experimentation in social work education and practice. It was, I felt, time to fulfil this purpose by narrating what the project had accomplished, the odds it had faced, and the lessons that had been learnt.

An advisory group was set up to help me think through the new project, and it advised me to 'write what is in your head', but 'do not make this a kitchen sink and throw everything into it'. This meant collecting data from my memories, thoughts, and reflections—one long self-indulgence. There was a sense that all the material would come from my thoughts, analyses, experience, and emotions. Was it not unreal or unfair to sit in a corner and think thoughts that may have little to do with reality or were irrelevant? And people would critique them. So I had to first weigh in the balance what was going to be described or narrated. The five themes that emerged from this encounter were the violated woman, the issue of violence against women, the state, the development of strategic alliances, and the role of social work education.

I have not considered writing to be my calling. I never dreamt of, or aspired to, writing stories. I wish I could write as I think or speak, full of sounds, gestures and facial expressions, reacting to my audience's responses communicated in the same manner. Storytelling and listening to stories have been a favourite pastime, but to write all this in an acceptable style has been most difficult. A memory is seen in the light of today, but capturing the meaning, relevance and value it had yesterday is a slippery task. Could it all be explored in depth?

As I wrote, whole new sections emerged—jostling thoughts and ideas, often losing their thread, glimmers lost in the sun like mirages in a desert. Associations made in the mind for recalling facts and places, and many, many words, thoughts and actions brought back memories of women, men, families, policemen, colleagues, and friends. I hasten to add that the memories were aided and abetted by diaries, notes, letters, presentations, papers, articles, discussions, and queries and answers from different sources.

The difficulties of the method I adopted were numerous. Reliving events coloured by emotions is an intensive and exhausting business. There were times when there was a blurring of boundaries, of happenings, of feelings. Recall, I realised, was layered by today's realities, frames of reference, and expectations. To mitigate the adverse effects of this, I repeatedly discussed and checked my memories with old colleagues and friends. As I explained to a young colleague,

> Yes, it is a personal account. But my thoughts are not wholly private. They are borne out by evidence on the ground. Yes, there is subjectivity. It gave me the space to assert my agency through the years, a principle central to my mentors, Freire, and feminist thinking.

Many, including members of my advisory group, wanted to know who my audience was. Whom was I addressing? Initially, my reaction was to say that you should tell me who has to be addressed. But as I settled into reading, writing and thinking, clarity emerged. My mind's eye sees me talking to young people, students, educators, workers, trainees, policemen, bureaucrats, and those in seats of governance.

The style of writing I have adopted is not linear. It is not propelled by either issues or chronology, but by an evolving learning cycle—themes as they emerged in my mind, one memory leading to another, with thoughts revolving round these memories. An activity began that we saw as an answer to the needs of women, experiences were gathered on the way, and there were actions and reactions that led to much more learning and many more activities. Aided by our participation in forums, meetings and wider debates, the experience was translated into training for the police and other stakeholders in the battle against violence on women.

In the process, I have discovered a lot about myself, my beliefs, my politics, my passions, my pleasures, the metaphors I live by, and the way I look at the world. I have also uncovered a capacity to read the emotional content underlying the intellectual, reasonable, or rational. There were insights that were enlivening and satisfying, but not all revelations were easy to swallow. There was a lot of talking and arguing with myself about what was real and what was not.

I was part of a team with two different persons at two different points in time in the Special Cell's journey. In the first few years, it was with Ashutosh Dharmadhikari, to set the project in motion, and then with Trupti Jhaveri, from 1997 till today. On reflection, these partnerships of accountability to women, our shared sense of purpose and convictions allowed for mistakes, arguments, debates, and a joint sense of responsibility. This definitely gave me emotional energy, and companions with whom discoveries, the little joys and problems of working with abused women and the police system could be shared. The knowledge that we could tune into each other's ideas and thoughts with just a word or a gesture while working in a highly volatile space gave us a feeling of reassurance. The bond created yielded dividends in work and aided the growth of self-identity. These have been elaborated in the following chapters. Writing this in a narrative style has allowed me to unfold happenings largely as they occurred, emphasising that work on the ground—indeed, life itself—is not linear but iterative.

The Special Cell's journey has been a silent one till date, in that it has not publicly acknowledged or recognised the people who have helped it. In this book, I have deliberately used names and designations while noting the different contributions at different levels that fostered the Special Cell's work and made it more visible. Another important influence on the writing and style has been the emotions that this going back in time has evoked. I often experienced a complete immersion in the past and relived our struggles with the state. Even as I wrote, I was aware that these wrangles are an ongoing affair, which upset and unsettled me, raising doubts in my mind about the work put in in the past 30 years. What had we achieved? Why continue to battle with the government? What was there to write about when we do not seem to have moved very far? Why chronicle the skirmishes with the mindsets of the powerful in the state? But we continue to work, telling ourselves that perhaps this is exactly the reason why we need to push forward, and also chronicle the journey.

I have written this in four parts. Chapter 1 briefly introduces the context of the Special Cell in 1984 and what led to it, my meeting points with the context, and the context of the writing project. Chapters 2–4 focus on the doings and the explanations—or on what we did and why we did it. It also tries to clearly acknowledge the roles played by other stakeholders. Chapter 5, or the Conclusion, reviews the impact of the Special Cell's work on creating access to socio-legal mechanisms to stop violence against women today. Finally, in the Timeline, I attempt to pull the common threads of what the experience has enabled us to learn, and what we have actually learnt. This has been an exercise in self-reflection.

2

Setting the Stage

Proposal for the Special Cell

In mid-1984, the academic year was nearing its end and I was set to complete my term as assistant lecturer at TISS. The University Grants Commission (UGC) had decided to discontinue assistant lecturer posts in 1983. Professor Apte wanted me to continue working with the department of family and child welfare, and offered me the option of initiating a field action project. One idea was to set up a coordination council for child welfare services in Mumbai city, and the other was to work on the issue of violence against women in the offices. I chose the latter. A blue 'noting sheet' was written on this to the then director of the institute, Dr A. Desai. She preferred my developing the project on coordinating child services, but I declined, as it was not my area of interest. The choice was basically between work with women and work with children. Having spent my childhood as a single child with my grandparents, the adult world was more fascinating and absorbing to me.

During my graduate course, women's studies were not a part of the curriculum. In my first job in a slum community, Korba Mithaghar in Wadala, I largely interacted with young men to develop youth groups on the lines of Freiren thought. Although working with women was only a very small part of the venture, it acquainted me with the stark realities of women's lives. The postgraduate course at TISS was also free of women, except for Professor S. Chitinis's course on child rearing. It captured my imagination, summoning up memories of my upbringing. In a way, it heightened my consciousness, making me realise once again that society at large considered women inferior, and did not value them or treat them with dignity. The instructional method was for students to read women's autobiographies, and present them in class for further discussion. The narratives made us uncomfortable, angry and rebellious, and our way of coping with this was to smile, smirk and laugh, so much so that Professor Chitins rebuked us for making merry in the classroom and asked if we really comprehended what was being talked about.

I cannot very clearly point out where my interest in working with women emerged, except that in my house, all the women were valued, loved, and given all that made us feel warm and secure. My mother and grandparents were my main society, and it was often said in the household that women must be treated with dignity and respect. No behaviour that was not respectful of my grandmother or the other women was accepted. In the external world of extended family, school and schoolmates, I noticed and registered the different ways in which people interacted with women and spoke of them. This was encoded in nuances of caste, gender and class, which were markedly different from the ways at home.

Soon after my graduation, Professor Apte invited me to join her in a voluntary women's organisation, Swadhar, which worked on violence against women. This was my first step towards understanding the larger women's movement of the time, which was wrestling with this issue. The idea appealed to me. This meant writing out a proposal and a letter to the Commissioner of Police (CP), Mr Julio Ribeiro, requesting an appointment to meet him (see Appendix 1). After calling repeatedly, we obtained an appointment at 3 PM on 8 March 1984, for the head of the department of family and child welfare, TISS (also referred to as the Institute). We sat in the waiting room of an imposing Gothic building and every time someone went in, I wondered why we were not being called. I discovered later that it had been the time the CP met the 'public', or ordinary citizens, who had grievances. Finally, it was our turn. Mr Ribeiro heard us, received the proposal, and assured us of his attention and a reply in a few weeks.

The proposal had been drafted by me, guided by Professor Apte, and edited by a classmate and friend, Kalpana Kaul. This proposal was the basis on which our work began. It contained the project's objectives, a request for administrative and infrastructural support for five years, and an explanation that funds would be raised by the

Institute. It was a far cry from the proposal writing of today, which has to have at least a baseline survey, impact indicators, outcomes, and an evaluation. On rereading the proposal, it occurs to me that the three things mentioned in it continue to be the pillars of our work even today—'professional social services to violated women', 'to give us the opportunity to pave the way for collaborative service between police and professional social work', and 'to realise women's efforts to be fully contributing members of society'.

We called the CP after a few days and he invited us for a meeting with his officers, this time in the morning. There were two police officers, one from the Juvenile Aid Police Unit (JAPU) and the other from the Social Service Branch (SSB). I remember one of them was a woman, who was very pregnant. The police officer was being kicked by her baby while she was saluting her seniors and sitting there in her uniform—seemed quite incongruous to me at the time. The meeting resulted in an agreement to set up a Project for Women in Distress in the CP's office. Since there was an SSB, the idea was put forth that the project be located in its office; however, the officer in charge insisted that the social workers had to be in a separate room. He explained that he did not want women and social workers to be exposed to the bad language used by the police. Perhaps he meant bad deeds as well. Or probably it was his way of drawing a line, making it clear that we were outsiders.

The CP, on the other hand, was welcoming, and there was no reason to complain. The decision at the end was that we would be given an independent space that suited the requirements of our work. A new office was to be created and furnished. The CP mentioned at the meeting that he was happy to welcome Professor Apte's initiative because he had sought the opinion of Dr M. S. Gore, retired director of TISS, who had praised her work in the field. Perhaps another reason for his considering the project was that the women's movement, championed by the media, was demanding that the police address rising crimes against women. This meeting took place in April, and we were committed to begin work in July after the convocation and summer vacation. Everything at TISS revolved around the academic calendar.

The second day of July 1984, a Monday, was when we began work on the Project for Women in Distress. It was also the beginning of our need to think on our feet in a new environment, the police system. The year ahead involved learning the police system and setting up systems for the Special Cell. The name 'Special Cell' was given by Mr Rebeiro. When he wanted to refer an application from the public or the police to us for intervention, he wrote, 'To Special Cell, Anjali Dave/Ashutosh Dharmadhikari'. The Project for Women in Distress was the TISS name, which the old guard at the Institute still uses, but it was the Special Cell within the police, and later among the public. The reasons for accepting this name were, first, it was given by the CP, and second, it fitted with the vocabulary of the police system, which we wanted to be a part of. Our social work had to blend with the needs of the people, not be obtrusive. The change in the board took longer.

Early Days and Approach

Ashutosh joined us in the second week of the Special Cell. As we came from different backgrounds, he and I brought two different approaches and ideological positions to the project. At first sight, all we had in common was the influence of Gandhian thought and a postgraduate degree in social work from TISS. But over a period of time, we discovered that our approaches were complementary, and that we often added to each other's thinking. Stimulating conversations, discussions and arguments pushed our mental boundaries and propelled our actions.

The intake register was the first system to be put in place. Categories in the register grew over the years due to the different kinds of cases handled, all to do with violence against women. The variety of files also grew, as different stakeholders had to be communicated with while dealing with violence against women in a police setting. For example, there were file copies of request letters to aggressors, letters to the police and lawyers, letters from collateral agencies, referral letters, and assurance letters, to name only a few. The learning process was gradual, and it took a dozen years to really streamline the organisation and administration of the Special Cell.

Home visits and collateral visits were a core component of the work. The police had accepted our request to provide and share infrastructural support. When the first case was referred to the Special Cell by the CP, Ashutosh took the lead to organise a home visit in a police vehicle. This reflected a valuable lesson learnt from Professor Apte's family counselling centre at the High Court—social service workers who lacked resources had to do everything they could to harness whatever help was available in the system. These visits yielded many benefits and confirmed the need for them. Yet, despite the need to respond quickly, we had to make sure we did not desert our desks whenever a senior policeman referred a case to us. We had to set times and days when we would be available to women who had heard of the new service, or to other people and organisations who wanted to meet us. As workers, we owed it to ourselves and to the police to be disciplined, especially within a system that was observing our work ethic closely. After all, we outsiders had been given prime space in the CP's office, new furniture, a telephone, and a writer (this person constituted the administrative assistance). Even leaving all of this aside, women whose rights had been infringed could not arrive to closed doors at a place that was purported to promote social justice.

Social work education teaches you—however simplistic it may sound—that you are to interact with people without letting your personal agenda affect the process. The same principle was applicable in our interactions with the police system. Our bargaining power for women had to be above board. So we were clear in our minds that the Special Cell would only respond to cases of violence against women, and that we would not use whatever little influence we had in the police system for anything else. When my teacher needed help to get a passport quickly, we told her what had to be done after finding out the procedure, but we did not go with her to the persons concerned. This was taking a high moral road, but it was imperative that we maintain a distance. Our motto was to use 'power' only in cases that involved violence against women. Women were our guiding force, and it was they who would establish our worth.

It should be borne in mind that our initial impression was that police powers were often misused, and we felt that we should not contribute to it. The police, on the other hand, believed that people were constantly trying to use them outside their roles and jobs. In the early days of the Special Cell, I needed a passport to go for a conference on family violence in Sri Lanka, where I was to make a presentation on our work. After much cogitation, I approached the CP. Interestingly, even before I could complete my hesitant sentence, he asked for the form he had to sign, called his secretary, and arranged for me to have the passport in seven days. We experienced the use and abuse of power all the time, in almost all transactions; it was a palpable presence in our everyday work. This made it evident that we needed to be highly disciplined, circumspect and discreet in our interactions with members of the police force. We were at all times cordial, pleasant and friendly, but there was very little personal interaction or private communication—no dropping into people's offices, no *chais*, and no aimless conversation or answers to personal comments and questions.

Introduction to the Police System

All our interactions with the police system—from simple office requirements to case-related work—gave us a peek into more than we had bargained for. The motor transport department had to be approached for the use of vehicles to make visits to homes, police stations, or collaterals, and the dispatch section to post our letters. The welfare section and computer section had their small but separate domains, and were our neighbours. The public works department had built our office in one of the buildings in the compound of the office of the commissioner, and installed the telephone and fans. All requests to the government for funds had to be routed through the department of monitoring and organisation. The transfer and promotion of the nodal officer, a Deputy Commissioner of Police, Head Quarters (DCP-HQ), to the Additional Commissioner of Police (Addl CP, Essential Services), opened up yet another world. We subsequently became acquainted with the lethal arms division, the police hospital, the building branch, and the provident fund and pension section, especially after women from police families approached us for help.

For sending a letter to other police officers in the city and state, there was the PN para office, where the police notice was published everyday. All the news of the police department, including leaves, transfers and deaths, had to be reported here for them to be official. The Special Cell was also reported in the police notice, granting us legitimacy in the system. Call letters—the name was adopted from the system—requesting that aggressors come to the Special Cell for a meeting had to be printed and posted from the police office. This is how we discovered the duplicating machines that stencilled the letters. Permissions were needed for the use of government resources from each department. All this, and more, required dealing with police officers in different capacities, to all of whom we explained our purpose. Our readiness to absorb new thoughts and influences gave us new insights and knowledge, even as we held steadfastly to women and to social work values and principles.

Continuous engagement with the police in a variety of situations and contexts acquainted us with their world and thought processes. They could use the law creatively, and harness police powers to deal with different cases. Sections of the Indian Penal Code (IPC) and the Criminal Procedure Code (CrPc) could be adroitly deployed, especially when they decided to help a case along. This taught us to include sections and principles of the law in our work. The process was tricky, and we sometimes got it wrong. But as time went by, things became clearer, and we found pathways in the law to assist women. One of the first discoveries was that Sections 107–114 of the CrPc—used to maintain peace in the community—could be used to stop domestic violence, especially if it spilled out and disturbed the neighbourhood. These sections gave the police quasi-judicial powers to bring peace between warring partners in a marriage or a family. Another realisation came while working with the police on cases involving Section 498A of the IPC. This showed us that arrest at the first instance was not a good practice in policing; however, the police had to do so on many occasions to appease the complainants.

Being a woman, my interactions with the women clerks and officers in the CP's office helped me to understand the system from a different angle. They gave me an idea of the problems and concerns of women working in a large government workplace, like the police department. For one, the women's toilets for the administrative and police staff were pathetic, to say the least. They were leaky, oddly designed and non-functional, and situated in ill-ventilated and poorly maintained spaces, which had been reclaimed and remodelled in accordance with the whims of individuals who happened to be in decision-making positions at different times. Women police officers used these spaces round the clock as places to rest, change, or let their hair down after a chaotic day of work. Senior women officers sometimes got a room of their own, but they had to belong to the Indian Police Service, or at least be a Deputy Commissioner of Police or Assistant Deputy Inspector General.

The ranks in the police were gradually comprehended, some because sympathetic police officers enlightened us and others because of awkward experiences. We learnt that a senior police officer visiting a police station always sits in the chair of the highest ranked officer there. His place in a car is across the driver in the back; however, if he is travelling in a jeep, he sits next to the driver. It was a huge break in formality when the CP took us in his car to visit the Mantralaya to watch a film on the police. Before setting off, the orderlies avoided eye contact till the CP told them to allow us into his car. Position, protocol, rules, authority, and power were seldom explained to us in words. We understood more through behaviour, the way we were treated in different spaces, our observations, and through answers to our questions.

The Special Cell Reaches Out

The CP held a routine press conference and also met individual journalists, to whom he mentioned that a Special Cell had been set up. This brought a few of the journalists our way. We were interviewed on TV programmes on a few occasions, while on others, we were invited to scrutinise the content of programmes to ensure that they did not foster violence against women. All this led to an increasing number of women approaching the Special Cell—more than 200 in the very first year.

The Special Cell had, in a sense, been a demand of the women's movement. The campaign against violence on women had demonstrated that the police notwithstanding, more had to be done to help women. The police had a heavy responsibility, but the role they played left much to be desired. What was seen as violence against women by women's organisations was viewed as marital conflicts by the police. These were to be resolved either by the women themselves, or by the police 'counselling' them. The experience of women's activists and organisations was that the police routinely discouraged criminal complaints, or simply sidestepped allegations. Apart from visiting every police station, introducing ourselves, and informing them of the new Special Cell, we contacted and visited women's organisations, since one of our objectives was to function as a liaison between them and the police. This led to meeting each other's workers, and sharing concerns and perspectives. More importantly, it taught us about the approaches, strategies, and relationships to be built for working on violence against women.

We were largely met with hope, encouragement, and a readiness to cooperate, although it was obvious that people would be keeping an eagle eye on what we did. Our interactions made us conscious of the need to build a critical understanding of the police as a force, which was popularly perceived as an agency of official high-handedness. We also encountered sharp criticism from some quarters for working with the state, the sceptics seeing it as co-option and being very wary about our ideas. We encountered the power and authority of the state on a daily basis and were quite aware of its potency, but we were also strongly convinced that social workers in the police system could work more effectively for the welfare of battered women. As a matter of fact, this strategic position enabled us to steadily expand the scope of our work and build relationships with different stakeholders. I cite a few examples to back this statement.

Project Help

Dowry deaths were increasing in Mumbai city. Women's organisations had become increasingly aware of the importance of dying declarations in investigations, the inability of victims to talk due to medical and social constraints, and the police's inept handling of these situations. In 1987, this became the basis for an experiment, with a hospital, women's organisations, the police, and the Special Cell coming together. The experiment was initiated and coordinated by the Special Cell, with the CP, Mr D. S. Soman, directing the police, and the municipal commissioner of Mumbai issuing a request for co-operation. Attempts were made to draw in the social work department of the hospital, but it was hesitant, perhaps because it meant working beyond duty hours, or because they were unwilling to work with activists with different perspectives.

Women's organisations were on call at Sion Hospital on rotation. Police at the casualty ward of the hospital were to call the minute they learnt that a woman with burns had been brought in. The women activists were to reach the hospital to support the woman in question, her children and her family, and the police were to intervene in the interests of the woman. The project ran for four months, yielding many useful lessons, before it was wound up. Among the findings was that medical emergency took precedence over everything else. Yet, the police and the medical team had to be alert to social and legal implications, something a new entrant could not do in an emergency situation. Besides, working with women who had suffered severe burns was difficult and painful, and not everyone could do it. The victims were often not in a position to talk, and the scene was charged with emotions, making any reasonable conversation with family members or others almost impossible. Lastly, the police were unable to provide logistical support to or coordinate with the women's organisations at the required moments (due to limited human and material resources), rendering them helpless when calls for help came at night.

This project was one of the first to call attention to the need for services in public hospitals to help abused women; such services, even now, are essentially available in only one hospital in Mumbai city.

Playing the Mediator

When women began accessing the services of the Special Cell, word of mouth was the most effective mechanism for referrals.

The network included former clients, women's organisations, voluntary organisations, the police, hospitals, and members of the public who themselves did not want to, or could not, intervene in cases of violence. While extending the work of the Special Cell, we built relationships with women's organisations and individuals working there. The fact that we were a young man-woman team evoked a fair amount of goodwill, and many felt we should be given encouragement and support for doing what we were.

Our objective—acting as a liaison between the police and women's organisations—led us to assist in police help reaching the people concerned. In one such case, the Women Centre approached us for help after a mother complained that she could not meet her daughter, who was being confined to her husband's house. We formed a group of Special Cell and Women Centre workers, and along with the family, went to the area the daughter lived in. When we got in touch with the neighbours, they said that it would be very difficult to see the daughter because her in-laws would not let her even come to the front door. One of them said:

> She is treated worse than a servant; her own child does not recognise her as the mother. The only time she goes out is to fetch the child from school, and that too is closely monitored.

This made us realise that social workers or not, we would not be welcome in the house. Seeking the help of the police seemed to be the only option.

It took the entire afternoon to convince the police, despite the mother giving a statement that her daughter was being wrongfully confined. At last, 15 policemen in two vehicles set out with us towards the house the daughter was in. As we neared the area, the police discovered that it was outside their jurisdiction. There were heavy sighs and a move to withdraw. It was almost 7 PM, and the Special Cell team had to try to convince the police all over again to continue. We even had to say that we would have to talk to their senior officers (we had an authorisation letter issued by the CP, and had been introduced to the zonal and regional police heads in the city). Our cajoling finally impelled them to move. By way of abundant precaution, they parked their vehicles far from the building and removed their uniform shirts. Guided to the house by the mother and women activists, the police rang the bell. It was now past 7.30 PM. The door was opened by the husband, his family members close behind him. It was apparent that they suspected something was amiss, but they did not resist us.

The police requested that the daughter be called out to meet her mother. After a wait of 10 minutes, she came out—pale, freshly washed, and wearing pearls. The small and thin woman sat on a sofa, away from us all. We asked her how she was and she responded that she was fine; however, her nervous gestures betrayed her anxiety. The visit culminated in us negotiating with the husband's family to allow the woman to visit the Special Cell the next day. This was intended to convey to the family that there were people who were aware the woman was being harassed, and that they could not hope to get away with their harassment.

This was an instance of learning to work together, of understanding the boundaries of each organisation and the individuals working in them when it came to dealing with violence against women. When we reported this case to the CP, he brought to our attention the need to exercise caution at all times in emotionally charged situations, particularly when working with the police system. The next day, the woman and her husband met Special Cell workers, and he assured us his wife would be treated in a better manner. None of the three actors involved—the mother, the Women Centre, and the daughter—returned to the Special Cell for help. The Special Cell had played its role of a liaison, or a conduit, connecting the different parties and gaining the mother access to her daughter. Social workers in the police system had been able to persuade the police to respond to a complaint of domestic violence and extract a promise of good behaviour from the husband—their role in the case ended there. This brought home the different roles that could be played by the Special Cell within the police set-up.

Shelter Pact

Bapnu Ghar, a shelter home run by a women's organisation, was considered to have a traditional outlook. The Special Cell occasionally referred cases to it because of the paucity of shelters in the city. This gradually grew into a relationship of acceptance and mutual respect. Its Superintendent and Committee recognised that we would continue intervening in cases with the Special Cell approach, while Bapnu Ghar's role would be to provide shelter. The welfare of women whose rights had been disregarded was our common goal, and they were willing to allow room for 'young people's new ideas'.

To digress a bit, a well-known woman lawyer, Flavia Agnes, once remarked, 'I feel sorry for you young people having no romance; all the rosy-eyed romance being taken away from you.' Needless to say, the part left unsaid at the end was, 'by working in the Special Cell'.

Educative Encounters

Commissioners of Police, from Mr Ribeiro to the many others who followed him, nurtured, mentored and supported the Special Cell teams. They created opportunities, educated us about the system through their experiences, and continue to do so to this day. Every request for help or suggestion was responded to with a certain amount of alacrity, and rarely did anybody demur to put resources behind an idea.

A student of social work was placed in the Special Cell for field-work in 1996, when Mr Satish Sahani was the CP. This student was very upset after visiting a police station in the northern suburbs of Mumbai. He was also indignant about the way the police had behaved in a case, and wanted the higher authorities to take note of it. We talked about this with him and also brought it to the CP's attention. The CP met the student and accepted a letter he gave him (the supervisor had worked with the student on the letter). This demonstrated the police's ability to respond to a variety of situations in the course of their work, including assuaging the feelings of an idealistic young man.

A few months later, a Special Cell worker paid a visit to the same police station and received a rousing welcome. She was profusely thanked for having brought about much-needed changes in conditions at the police station by bringing its inadequacies to the notice of the CP. The student who had prompted all of this heard of the positive fallout later, but he felt there had been a value to his educative interaction with the police and appreciated the openness that the CP had shown. This had been possible because of the person Mr Sahani was, and the healthy relationship that the Special Cell had built with the police system.

Setting up Systems to Work with Abused Women

The first case referred to us had to do with the wife of a police constable. Mr Ribeiro called me on the morning of the first day of the Special Cell. I entered the imposing room of the CP, rather self-conscious and anxious to do well. After giving me a brief background of the case, he looked at me enquiringly—what could I do for her? Nothing very bright occurred to me, but training, experience, and the need to put my best foot forward made me say, 'It depends on what she wants. Let me talk to her and find out what we can do.' This basic doctrine of social work—self-determination—became our guiding principle over the years.

The norm in most official spaces is that people submit an application—a letter enclosing a request for help—when they want to avail themselves of a service. This woman had written an application to the CP, and he marked it to me. This placed on record the fact that the woman had approached the police, and that the matter had been referred to the Special Cell. It also gave us her permission to take action on her request. We understood over time that this was important in our context, because we were social workers operating within a formal structure that was bound by the law. Any trespass in areas or spaces such as a family's private life was out of the question. As social workers, we had to remain conscious of our context as we set up systems and practices. Obtaining the written permission of women to intervene was one of them.

We discovered that the written word was also important to the women who came to the Special Cell. It made them aware that they were taking an important step by challenging the violence against them, and that they were moving out of the context of family and community into the world of the law and government—the 'outside'. This led to a rise in their expectations, heightened their sense of justice, and made them willing to assert their rights in a more visible manner. At the individual level, when a woman writes, she articulates her problem, and mentions what she would like an outside agency to do for her. She thus takes a step towards action to remedy her situation. So this practice—of women submitting written applications, in which they specified their problem and the help they would require from the Special Cell—was developed.

There were critics who said that the women were mostly illiterate, and therefore it was unrealistic to expect them to carry out 'official' tasks. This, to my mind, was the first obstacle to setting up systems where women counted. Our training and belief in self-determination said that we could not treat all women as helpless victims who only deserved pity. Nor could we consider them fools who could not think for themselves. We could not take over their lives. Women who wanted support could be helped to take the first few paces, but they had to decide the direction in which they wanted to go. We felt that our procedures had to reflect our beliefs and convictions. If we believed that violence against women was partly because society did not permit them to take charge of their lives, we could not allow it to continue. A practice that dealt with women not only as injured parties but also as independent individuals had to be put in place.

An oral narration of a woman's difficulties brings alive the situation to the social workers and allows them to emote with her, but also has the potential to be interpreted erroneously or forgotten. A written account documents her history of violence, her perceptions, and the help required, giving social workers a clear idea of what has to be done. We requested women to write their applications themselves. If they could not do so, they could get someone in their family, or a friend, to do it for them. However, we found that many women interpreted this as us wanting a typed letter, and got their applications done by professional typists after paying a fee. We were taken aback, before deciding that we had to make the best of the literate environment we were in. The Special Cell office was next to the computer section, which had many well-educated constables who were curious about our work and empathetic to it. They soon began volunteering to write for the women. This contributed to making conditions more conducive in the workplace. Often, something done on commonsensical grounds connected to the values we held, and also strengthened the relationship we were building with the police system.

Domestic violence was a well-known phenomenon in this environment, and this was probably why women did not shy away from talking about their problems to strangers while getting their applications written by them. Of course, the more delicate and private details were only shared orally with Special Cell workers. And here, the principle of confidentiality ruled. All this needs to be understood in the context of women who found themselves in a formal world often alien to them, where the written word carried a lot of weight and value. While only vaguely aware of the power of the written word, they began to draw power and confidence from it once the process was set in motion. We understood this as we began treating each woman as a unique individual, and many positive things soon followed. Acknowledging that women have, and must have, agency, and that we were committed to address violence against them, naturally meant that they had to be treated as individuals in their own right, deserving dignity, respect and self-esteem.

More often than not, women wrote about the pain of being abused—physically and emotionally—by their husbands and in-laws. After giving in her application, a woman would typically spend hours talking to a Special Cell worker, detailing incidents of violence, and describing her helplessness, before saying that she wanted to be reconciled with her abusive spouse and his family. She would ask the worker to call her husband and threaten him, so that he would stop harming her, repeating that she wanted to live with him. I often thought this was out of helplessness, and to get it straight in my mind, asked women why they wanted to be with their violent husbands—was it just because they were their husbands, or because they liked them as persons? There were many who resignedly said, 'What else can I do?', indicating that the marriage was their livelihood. Many others said, 'He is a good man. It is only this, that, or the other that makes him angry and violent. He cares for me and my child.' In short, these situations involved a complex set of factors, making it nearly impossible for a beaten wife to pack her bags the next day and leave her husband.

This gave rise to the practice of the first meeting, where a woman, usually accompanied by members of her family or friends, told her story to a Special Cell worker. Having heard her out, the worker would ask her to begin thinking about what she wanted to do, and suggest that she put it all down in an application. Upon receiving the application, the Special Cell would send a call letter to the person identified as the aggressor, requesting him to meet us in our office. Most husbands or male partners came to the Special Cell because of its address, and not because they saw a possibility of resolving the situation. Some came alone, not wanting anyone to know that they were being accused of being abusive. Others came with a family member or even a lawyer, bringing the power of the law to counter the hostility they perceived in the call letter.

Table 2.1: Residence at the Time of Approaching the Special Cell

	Total no. of women			
Residence at the time of approaching Special Cell	**Year 2008 (N=129)**	**Total number 2,334**	**Total number 2,930**	**Total number 303**
In the matrimonial home	16.3	21.5	21.3	19.7
Staying with parents	70.5	63	49.4	32.7
Staying with relatives	2.3	4.7	0.7	2.8
Staying in shelter home	.8	0.3	0.3	1.5
Staying independently	4.7	9.2	9.4	INA
INA	3.1	0.3	11.4	35.1
Any other	2.3	1	7.3	
Percent	100.0	100	100	100

Note: INA— Information Not Available.

Source: Apte 2004, Dave and Solanki 2000, Haryana 2008, Special Cells 1997, for columns 2, 3, 4, and 5, respectively.

After the initial meeting with the woman, she was asked to call the Special Cell to check if her aggressor had responded to our letter. Most of the women who approached the Special Cell were living outside their marital homes (see Table 2.1). The letter gave the man a week's notice, and having committed herself to action, the woman waited in hope and trepidation. But rarely did women withdraw their application in this period. This was because they had already reached a stage where they could tolerate no more, and wanted an end to the violence. Data informs us that women reached out to the police when they perceived a threat to their marriage, to their foetus or child, or their own lives—33.9 per cent of the women who came to the Special Cell for help had already approached the police (Dave and Solanki 2000), and 48.20 per cent of them had availed themselves of police help (Apte 2004).

The desire for a better life and the determination to struggle for it was very strong in those who came to the Special Cell. These women were survivors; more than 98 per cent of the applications received at the Special Cell came directly from abused women. Visiting the Special Cell and interacting with the workers there gave them the courage and support they needed to confront their aggressors (Table 2.2).

Table 2.2: What Women Liked about Special Cells

Sr. No.	What women liked about Special Cells which made them come after the 1st interaction	(N= 303)	Percentage
1	Approach to Problem-solving	234	77.2
2	Workers' explanation of my context of violence	179	59.1
3	Atmosphere in the Special Cells	95	31.4
4	Focused time and attention given to me	210	69.3
5	Felt someone was with me	233	76.9
6	Woman can come here alone	117	38.6
7	No fees are charged	72	23.8
8	I am understood as a woman	134	44.2
9	Woman are given priority	86	28.4
10	I was given encouragement to deal with my struggles and I felt hopeful	222	73.3

Source: Apte 2004.

When a woman talks about a violent man in her life and the havoc he has wreaked, a social worker tends to form a mental image of this person. In an early case, a woman came to me with a recently broken nose and hand, and a history of abuse. She described the incidents of violence and the use of physical force by her husband that had culminated in these injuries. I sent a letter to the husband and waited for him on the appointed date, all prepared to deal with a tall, well-built and violent man with a fierce moustache. The man who finally entered the room was small and thin, a little unsure of himself, and nervous about having been called to the CP's office. I recall that he and I were about the same size. Odd though this may have seemed, the man was there with his version of the 'truth', and I settled down to listen. The practice that emerged in the Special Cell was to listen to the men who had been summoned, and then call a joint meeting with their spouses or partners, if that was what was desired.

Joint meetings were mostly set up on the insistence of women, who wanted arbitration to help them negotiate better terms for living with their abusive husbands. A joint meeting allowed for an interaction between the couple on neutral ground—neutral at least to the extent that it was held within a police station, and a Special Cell worker was present to ensure the women were not unfairly pressured. These meetings were meant to enable the partners to ask each other questions and obtain answers. They could explain their views on the episodes of violence, and clarify how things stood with regard to their intentions for the future. They also allowed the women to see their husbands in a different surrounding, and helped them to judge how sincere their promises were. The Special Cell worker could assess the emotional responses of the couple to the situation, and evaluate the environment—family and community—they would be in (Dave and Dharmadhikari 1987). During individual meetings, a Special Cell worker would help to build a woman's ability to think critically, aid self-reflection, and assess her needs and desires while she decided on her immediate and long-term future. For the joint meetings, a worker would prepare her with the arguments necessary to negotiate a non-violent reconciliation.

In the joint meetings, the Special Cell worker often became an arbitrator, a defender of all that was non-negotiable, and an observer, all rolled into one. This was akin to highly skilled tightrope walking. Adherence to a simple principle—treating all persons at the table equally—was the key to doing so successfully, although this was easier said than done. However, this was necessitated by the large majority of women who wanted to maintain their relationships with their men. They believed, and often explained, the purpose of life as 'webs of relationships'. The Special Cell's mission was promoting women's well-being and supporting them to achieve it. If this meant working with the men in question, however distasteful it was in some instances, then it too had to be a part of the Special Cell's mandate. Joint meetings were not meant for addressing marital discord alone. They were also held when women complained about their own families, groups within the community, and employers. Yet another occasion arose when men wanted to marry women who had been prostitutes. In such cases, the woman wanted the Special Cell to vet her suitor and be by her side if he abused her.

The Framework, Home Visits, and Community Groups

The Special Cell's initial interactions with women raised doubts and discomfiting questions regarding how it could go about supporting them. This led us to think of the vision of society envisaged in the Constitution, and a loose formulation of the Special Cell's boundaries emerged. Social work principles, ethics and values would form the backbone of the Special Cell's work with women. This would be aided by our growing understanding of feminism and the law, leaving us with a large landscape to work in. This framework acquired sharper definition after further interaction with women's organisations, women activists, lawyers, and the police. To a journalist's question as to what I would have done had I been a feminist in 1984–85, I only had this honest response, 'Not having read enough, I am unable to say.' This nudged me into reading more, and interacting with the women's movement and its activists beyond the immediate need for developing a service for distressed women in the police system. What it all added up to was a better grasp of the theoretical issues involved, which translated into sound practices at work.

There were also women who wanted a place to talk about their problems, discuss them, and reflect on their situation. They did not want arbitration or negotiations with their aggressors, but wanted to get material help for themselves and their children. This was a legitimate request; however, as we were espousing self-determination and women's rights, it took us a while to understand this. We realised over time that an organisation's practice cannot become the only approach, and that we as an organisation had to constantly learn because we did not know, or have, all the answers. We had to gradually develop our capacity, as well as our contextual tools and strategies, to work in the 'real' world of abused women. The women who came to the Special Cell were also responsible for this because they pushed and prodded us, and were not afraid to ask critical questions. In a manner of speaking, the understanding, patience, needs, and desires of the women who had experienced violence played a large role in keeping us on the straight and narrow path.

Home visits were a tool we were familiar with from our education in social work, and a critical component of the work with individuals. Our first home visit took place in the third week of the Special Cell. The complainant was a woman lawyer from an upper middle-class family in one of the oldest parts of the city. She had multiple grievances, including non-action by the police. The case was referred to us by the CP, who wanted us to assess the gravity of the situation and learn what the family dynamics were. Within two hours of the referral, a police vehicle was organised for us to make the home visit.

Our home visits in a police vehicle always intrigued onlookers. Nobody really expected two young persons, reasonably pleasant and cordial, to emerge from a police vehicle. But the confusion had the effect of decreasing the suspicion with which a police vehicle was viewed. When a door was opened, we explained that we were social workers from an office in Crawford Market (the area in which the CP's office and the Special Cell were located), and that we had received an application. Entry to homes was rarely refused, and most families understood who social workers were. They were also responsive to our enquiries, usually about the aggressor and the family, and were quick to express opinions about what had happened. This was what happened on our first visit as well.

Home visits were mainly carried out when an aggressor did not respond to our letters. They were also made if an aggrieved woman, an aggressor, or his family insisted on them. Visits were sometimes undertaken to meet neighbours and other members of the community when the issue was complicated, and we needed a better understanding of the immediate environment. Collateral visits were made to police stations, offices, employers, and schools when a woman and her children's links to them or their assets had to be rebuilt. Home visits were carried out by Special Cell workers. Although policemen could help, they were bound by the law, and could not barge into homes without being liable to the charge of trespass. We, too, understood the value of measured interaction in every case. We had to be careful not to infringe on a man's legal and human rights while fighting for his partner's rights. Women and their grievances were central to our work, but we had to stay within the bounds of the law, ethics, and feminist and social work values. We had to often remind ourselves to keep the personal aside and not play to the gallery. We had to be conscious of our own politics, while remaining alive to the dictum that the personal is political.

The women often acted as our guides on home visits, and accompanying them at the initial stage of the intervention gave them emotional support and boosted their confidence. Later, the Special Cell worker would give them reference letters to help them navigate the offices they would have to visit to avail themselves of whatever benefits were available. Our orientation visits to police stations had introduced the police to the new service, and telephone calls were made to the local stations in whose jurisdictions abused women lived, to make them aware that we expected help and action if it was sought. This was a message to both the women—that they were capable of working independently on their problem—and the police—that the harassed women were not alone, that we had studied their cases, and that there was a legal role for the police to play. On certain occasions, we had to visit police stations, but these visits were to enquire about inaction, to discuss legal implications, to explore options, and to understand the fine line between cognisable and non-cognisable offences. These exchanges sharpened our understanding of the law and its application, from the perspective of both the individual and the police.

Over the months, we realised the influence that multiple factors—especially the social structure and hierarchy—exerted on the issue of violence against women, and the role played by personal beliefs in the interpretation of laws to do with women's rights. There was an ongoing debate in the media on violence against women, which focused mainly on dowry deaths. The word 'dowry' was used by women and their lawyers in their complaints to garner attention and action, while the police were wary of it for fear of media attention. While the law on dowry was inadequate to respond to the complex realities of women's situations, it became the job of the Special Cell to disaggregate the information provided by women to identify the issues on which legal action could be taken, particularly by the police. We were simultaneously decoding and translating the lives of abused women into a form that the police and the law could handle, while relearning concepts and theories through our work with women from a range of castes, classes, regions, and religions. The true meanings of terms such as society, social structure, oppression, politics, and rights were palpably visible in the dealings between men and women at the Special Cell.

Women have clearly defined roles and responsibilities in their families and communities. Every religion and community has its set of rules on marriage and divorce. Although all come under the umbrella of religious laws, practices differ between sects and sub-sects. A large number of the women who came to the Special Cell had resorted to their community mechanism of arbitration, but were not satisfied with what had been meted out to them. Many women wanted their panchayats to be included in the arbitration process at the Special Cell, to guard against excommunication from the community. So working with panchayats and *jamat*s, and negotiating with them on behalf of the women, became one more practice of the Special Cell. Over time, these panchayats, *jamat*s, unions, and other community-based groups referred cases to the Special Cell for resolution, and participated in negotiations when the women so desired, thus building one more strategic relationship.

Dealing with a Range of Problems

Emoting with the abused women was empowering for both social workers and the women; however, the Special Cell's work required a lot of emotional energy, and some discipline was called for. We used to say in the office, 'You cannot cry so much that the woman has to say "It's all right, don't worry, I will take care of myself"'. More than 80 per cent of the cases the Special Cell dealt with in the initial years had to do with domestic violence (Apte 2004; Dave and Solanki 2000; Special Cells 1997). From the very beginning, though, women came to us with a wide range of problems, and we gained a more complete understanding of women's position in society while working on these. I enumerate some of them below.

A prostitute wanted to know if we could help her protect her income from her *gharwali* (mistress). 'Now that she is growing older, her income is decreasing, and she wants to save more for herself,' she said. She came for a couple of discussions on how she should go about it, but did not want the Special Cell to take any direct action. Upon reflection, it was brave of her to state what her work was and fight for her rights. What probably brought her back for discussions was the fact that we did not moralise or attempt to 'rehabilitate' her.

A women's organisation asked for the Special Cell's assistance to get the police to intervene when a woman who was a lesbian was locked up in her family home. This was a difficult proposition to explain to the police, or get their agreement on. So we built up the argument that the woman was being detained against her will and that her mobility was being restricted, both of which are violations of her human rights and against the law. This was the only way of convincing the police to solve the problem. Use of the goodwill we had built over time, reasoned arguments, and an appropriate use of the law were crucial to our work.

Another prostitute was being wooed by a client who wanted to marry her. She needed a place to discuss her thoughts and anxieties. She had drifted into prostitution after a bad marriage, and did not want to walk into another exploitative relationship. She knew there was the possibility of her being vulnerable if she married.

What she wanted was a Special Cell worker's help in assessing the man. The underlying message she wanted to convey was that she had people to rely on, who would stand by her if he abused her. The Special Cell often played this role of 'passive challenger'. What some women required was a sympathetic ear, a validation of their thoughts and perspectives, and the assurance that the Special Cell would be there as a repository of their rights if they had to turn to it in the future.

A woman had been separated from her husband. The latter did not want reconciliation, nor did he want to pay her maintenance. She alleged that he had raped their 10-year-old daughter. We began investigating and found that she was not only reluctant to reveal any details, but she also did not want to file a criminal case against the man for the alleged rape of her daughter. She visited the Special Cell twice or thrice, but did not come after that. The former husband responded to our letter, and gave us his explanation on why the accusation of rape had been made. Ultimately this remained an 'incomplete' interaction. We did not pursue the woman as our practice was to leave it to the women to decide the course of their lives. This may have been a cry for help that we did not understand, but we did not have the means to analyse the behaviour and motivations of those who came to us. It also pointed to the limited social resources and legal options that women have at their disposal, including 'having only the oppressor as a role model' (Freire 1972).

Girl child abuse in the family, essentially incest and rape, were often part of women's stories. They alluded to it and connected it with their present abuse, more specifically, their emotional health. Seminars and a report published in 1990, the year of the girl child, have echoed these complaints of abuse by the women.

Family dynamics revealed a lot about the powerlessness of women caught in circumstances over which they had no control. For instance, this was stark in a case where an unmarried daughter's earnings supported her parents and younger siblings. But she had no say in anything, and felt that she was not only being used, but was also uncared for. In another instance, two daughters were being wooed by the same man. There were also men who had enticed the younger sisters of their wives, cynically turning their 'joking relationship' into an abusive one. And in one case, a grandmother wanted her granddaughter to procreate with her father so as to curtail costs in her old age.

A young man, his wife, and his family were ostracised by a panchayat because he had married a woman from another community. They were not allowed to interact with their relatives, or with anybody else in the community. They belonged to a fishing community where the men were away at sea for weeks, and so community support was essential for the women, children and elders at home. The young man's concern was that his family would not be able to access the social network for support. The panchayat's concern was related to the fate of unmarried women in the community, if more men married from outside it. The Special Cell explained the socio-legal position to the community members, making it clear that it was illegal and unconstitutional to ostracise anybody. Some of the members invited the Special Cell to a community meeting, but it was aborted when others learnt that social workers from the police were to attend it.

Mental Disorders, Open Files, and Assurance Letters

Young women came to the Special Cell to talk about relationship problems with their partners and parents. It almost always involved a family's disapproval of a woman's association with a certain man. Some had run away from home and wanted police protection from their parents. Others sought shelter or legal advice. They all believed that their right to make individual choices was being violated, and many had been subject to overt and covert violence—daughters had been detained in their homes, disallowed to communicate with their friends, and so on. Drugs, dating violence and 'voluntary prostitution' were some of the other problems that young people came to discuss. The Special Cell often served as a small but welcoming space for communication within the spartan environs of the large police office.

More than 80 per cent of the women who approached the Special Cell complained of mental violence, and a good many of them suffered from common mental disorders (Dave and Solanki 2000).

There were also a number of mentally disturbed women who frequented the Special Cell office. Most of them were single, on medication, and had minimal family support. They sat through the day talking to the workers, advised other women, and helped with simple chores. They refused to leave till the office closed. They had all initially come for help, but followed very little of what had been suggested. They had a past and a present, but were unwilling to share it. Some lived on the streets, and others on the fringes of their community or family. Our inability to address their issues highlighted a huge gap in our services. We could not do much beyond referring them to an empanelled psychiatrist, and training ourselves to work on the mental health concerns of abused women.

Then there was an assortment of people who came to enquire about what could be done with regard to some case they knew of—a girl being abused in the next house, a domestic servant being ill-treated, or a colleague being beaten by her husband. There seemed to be distress all around, which many noticed without knowing what could be done about it. Some wanted to know if the law could be used to do something. Helplessness and hope went hand in hand. Often, their talk about a friend, a colleague, or a cousin was a smoke-screen—they were really talking about themselves.

Most of the women who came to the Special Cell were concerned that their 'webs of relationships'—their strength and their weakness—were being affected. A woman's identity was inextricably linked to her marriage and her family. All her problems—sexual, economic, legal, mental, and emotional—were related to this. Changes in the hues of these difficulties were largely related to class, caste and social networks, and the emotional well-being of a woman's natal family. We found that several women from the middle and lower-middle classes came for help (BPP 1997; ES 2004; Haryana 2008; JVC 2000). There were, however, proportionately fewer women from amongst pavement dwellers and the poorer slums. The poorest of the poor had a different priority—they were doing whatever they could to survive the violence of poverty, which often masked the violence against women.

All of this contributed to the practice of the Special Cell not 'closing' any file—unlike in a police station or a court. Problems could recur or women could require some other help. We had to have an open door policy for women, and be a safe place that they could retreat to and talk openly about how they were being mistreated. This, perhaps, partly explains why women came to the Special Cell, and continue to do so.

Table 2.3: Learnings from Interactions with the Special Cell Worker

Sr. No.	What did she learn from her interaction with the Special Cell Worker	N=303	Percentage
1	Clarity of the problem	147	48.5
2	Importance of papers/documents	22	7.3
3	Importance of self/self-expression	21	6.9
4	Importance of taking decisions for oneself	72	23.8
5	Violence need not be accepted	34	11.2
6	Violence is a crime	55	18.2
7	That it is not my fault	39	12.9
8	My husband cannot abuse me	34	11.2
9	Information and alternative options	222	73.3
10	Any other	5	1.7

Source: Apte 2004.

Realising the importance of the written word in society, women would often say after negotiations, 'Ask him to give it in writing'. This reflected power—the power conferred on them by the Special Cell to question their partners. Men, who had so far not been challenged for abusing their partners, found themselves promising their commitment to peace in the presence of a Special Cell worker. The women, who mostly asked not to be beaten and to be maintained well, saw this as a fallback option. Soon, men, too, began asking the women to write down that they would be good wives and follow their instructions. Thus began the practice of writing assurance letters. The Special Cell played a critical role in this by ensuring that the content of the letters upheld women's dignity and self-respect.

An assurance letter became prime evidence in a court case. A young educated woman who had been harassed and beaten by her husband wanted to live with him in a non-violent marriage. They agreed on this, and he wrote that he would not abuse her, that they would reconcile their differences and live together. Three months later, the woman's parents came to the Special Cell to say that she had died under mysterious circumstances. The police had begun working on the case, and presumed it was a suicide. But this turned into a murder investigation when they read the application the woman had given to the Special Cell, which described the violence in her marriage. The assurance letter given by the husband implicitly accepted that he had been abusive. These documents led to a new line of enquiry, which saw evidence emerge from the site of the crime that pointed to the husband. He was eventually convicted of murder.

A Special Cell worker was called to the court as a witness in this case. This was new, because the Special Cell had a clear understanding with the police that it would not be drawn into the process of the law and courts. This was to ensure that social workers did not spend a large part of their time in the courts, like the police did. We also wanted to emphasise that social workers had a different set of skills and values to respond to violence against women. This had to do with the maxims of social work, and was not litigious. This was accepted in principle and supported in practice, but there have been cases involving murder, suicide and dowry deaths—few and far between—when Special Cell workers have had to be witnesses in court. Family court judges have in a few instances called Special Cell workers for discussions, or to present documents as evidence. We were compelled into these activities by women and their lawyers or families, although it was not mandatory to do so, till the Protection of Women from Domestic Violence Act came in 2005, and the Special Cell became a service provider.

All communication from the police to the Special Cell, which can be considered a Special Officer under the Bombay Police Act, is in the form of a request, and not an order. The CP had issued an 'authority letter' to the Special Cell in 1984 (see Appendix 3), and this procedure has been followed by all district superintendents of police in Maharashtra. The letters request others—such as the judiciary and women's organisations—to assist the Special Cell in its work on violence against women.

I conclude this part with three observations. One, the location of the Special Cell and the issue it takes on—violence against women—have allowed it to develop an identity of its own and function as a socio-legal mechanism that aids all distressed women who approach it. Two, the practices developed by the Special Cell over the years, on the basis of its experience in intervening in a wide variety of cases, have enabled it to develop a set of monitoring indicators to evaluate its performance. And three, the Special Cell serves as a model that can be replicated elsewhere, even in an expanded form, if need be.

Operation Outreach

What began as information sharing on the new initiative, the Special Cell, with women's organisations, the police and the media gradually spread to many community-based organisations and educational institutions. Invitations began coming in from women's organisations, community-based organisations, and non-government organisations (NGOs) to share the purpose of the Special Cell with their target audience. This, in time, grew into Special Cell workers being invited to be resource persons at seminars, training programmes, and sessions with the general public, especially women's groups. The workers began sharing their work experience, insights and information to combat violence against women. In 1986, we began organising training programmes for the police on violence against women and juvenile justice, drawing on resources at TISS.

Over the years, we have addressed a wide spectrum of people from different walks of life, dealing directly or indirectly with the issue of violence against women. This comprises the police at all levels across the country, including in training institutes; magistrates and judges; women and girls in communities and institutions; students; social workers; grassroots-level workers involved in programmes run by the government and by NGOs; women members of panchayats and zilla parishads; and government officials at the state and district levels. The learning acquired by Special Cell workers from their work with mistreated women, families, and the criminal justice system was reorganised to form a part of a preventive programme on addressing violence against women. Although an iterative process, this has furthered their growth and bettered their performance. Special Cell workers have participated in campaigns on women's rights, LGBT rights and the Domestic Violence Bill, and organised *melas* (fairs) for women. The Special Cell is now an integral part of the network of women and children's organisations that are committed to promote women's empowerment in society.

Collaborative Work

By being a member of various networks and forums, the Special Cell has joined hands with different organisations and groups to work on specific tasks and assignments. It has worked with a wide spectrum of organisations and groups that endeavour to promote women's rights, or at least prepare the ground for it.

- In a strategic alliance with the police to deal with violence against women, the Special Cell works with them in eight states, viz., Maharashtra, Rajasthan, Madhya Pradesh, Haryana, Gujarat, the erstwhile Andhra Pradesh, Delhi, and Orissa.
- It works with women's organisations to tackle child sexual abuse and violence against women, and to conduct *yuvati melas* (gatherings and fairs for women).
- Courts have appointed it to carry out social investigations, and Special Cell workers have been members on panels set up by family courts.
- It has served on sexual harassment committees in the police force and other government organisations.
- It has been part of committees set up by the state and the central government, especially the Ministry of Women and Child Development and Home, and UN organisations such as the United Nations Development Fund for Women

(UNIFEM) and the United Nations Population Fund (UNFPA).

- It works with women's commissions, both at the state and national levels.
- It has actively participated in programmes organised by the Lawyers Collective, the India Centre for Human Rights and Law, and the Commonwealth Human Rights Initiative.
- It cooperates with organisations working amongst minority groups, especially to aid victimised women.
- It has set up helplines, both with the police and voluntary organisations, and contributed to making films and documentaries on violence against women.

This collaborative work has been a recognition and validation of our core work, and has presented us with opportunities to learn from each other's work, ideologies and contexts. It has widened the horizons of Special Cell workers, who could share their thoughts and insights with a larger audience. It has also enlarged their networks and provided them with the impetus to move forward resolutely. The ability to relate, interact and communicate with people from diverse backgrounds and cultures has helped to enlarge their individual capacities, reinforcing their desire to create a more inclusive society. A belief that Special Cell workers have a distinct role and responsibility, but are also simultaneously individuals and members of society, has kept the flag flying high.

Numbers, Images and Impressions

Distressed women who look for assistance from the police and social organisations are largely drawn from the lower-middle and middle classes (Dave and Solanki 2000; Special Cells 1997). All these women, irrespective of class and caste, have a history of being abused. Between 1990 and 1997, a total of 2,930 women approached the Special Cell. While 58.4 per cent of them described physical violence, 83.5 per cent recounted mental violence (Dave and Solanki 2000). Their economic status, whether high or low, only aggravated matters. Housing was another bone of contention, and 42.9 per cent were not living in their matrimonial homes because of domestic violence (ibid.).

That violence against women is widespread in the country is obvious from the 2011 report of the National Crime Records Bureau (NCRB), which recorded 99,135 cases of a husband or his relatives subjecting a woman to cruelty—a crime under Section 498A of the IPC. This constituted 4.3 per cent of the total crimes under the IPC, and it had the highest number of registered cases of crime against women. Yet, the conviction rate was only 20.2 per cent. The third round of the National Family Health Survey (NFHS-3), conducted in 2005–06, reported that about 20 per cent of married women in the country between the ages of 15–49 had experienced violence from their spouses. About two-thirds of them described incidents that had occurred in the year of the survey. Among all women, married and unmarried, 34 per cent in the age group of 15–49 had experienced violence in their lifetime. In the case of married women who had experienced violence, 85 per cent reported that the perpetrator was the husband. In addition, 9 per cent of all women reported having faced sexual violence at some point in their lives, while 16 per cent of married women reported having been subject to emotional violence (IIPS 2007).

More recent numbers, such as the cases registered under the Protection of Women from Domestic Violence Act, 2005, only confirm the magnitude of violence against women, as well as their attempts to counter it. For instance, in Haryana, after Special Cells were opened and protection officers appointed in the 20 districts in November 2008, the number of women who approached them for help in the first year was 3,504. By March 2012, that number had swelled to 13,461 (RCIVAW-TISS 2013).

My mental image of those who came to the Special Cell in its early days is of sombre, anxious and tentative women, who tried to contain their agitation. But encouragingly, there was an air of expectation and hope about them. When a woman came in the first time, an effort was made to put her at ease before we asked her the reason for her visit. She would then tentatively begin narrating her story of abuse, which almost invariably included her being the target of violence by her spouse, and sometimes his family. There would also be the complaint that she was not being provided with enough money to look after the family and herself, and occasionally the allegation that her husband had deserted her (in more than 30 per cent of the cases). She would go on to say that she wanted her man to stop abusing her and give her what was adequate to live on, while insisting that she wanted to be reconciled with him. The emphasis was most often on material aspects, although her life was caught in a whirl of social norms and emotional struggles, and the misery of living with it. There was usually no direct reference to sex, sexual violence, or incompatibility, although some of this was sometimes implied, in words or through a studied silence.

A large part of a woman's emotional unrest was linked to her expectations from marriage remaining unfulfilled, and concerns about her physical health. The former found articulation in accusations such as: 'He has not bought me one blouse piece in all these years', or 'He has never taken me for an outing, not even for a film'. Or it would be something like: 'He never accompanies me to any social gathering with relatives or family'; 'He does not use good words with me, not one loving word'; 'He does not want sex with me'; or the other extreme, 'He only uses me for sex'. All this spoke of her not being valued or respected as an individual, even as she looked for an elusive emotional bond with her husband.

There was the pain of being rejected by the very person who, as a young girl, she had been told would shower her with love, affection and care. She had, in most cases, been held back by her natal family from fully developing an identity. Natal families tend to hold out the promise that marriage cures all ills, or that a woman's freedom lies in marriage. She had understood marriage to be of primary importance to women. The ultimate goal of a woman was to become a wife, and that of a man to become a worker, which usually determined their social status. Developmental psychologist Erik Erikson has maintained that a woman's very identity has to remain sufficiently flexible to allow her to adapt to her future husband and children (Lawrence 1999). A girl's life is always controlled and restricted, and her movements are closely supervised. These restrictions, which prevent her from straying into territory where she might run the risk of rendering herself less fit, intellectually or sexually, for marriage, serve as practice for what will eventually become her lot.

In the initial meetings, women did not speak directly of sexual relations. But it was alluded to in speech that was couched in socially acceptable language. Special Cell workers realised this when the subject was brought up by men in joint meetings through remarks such as: 'She is cold'; 'She does not allow sex'; 'She is always busy with the children'; 'She is inhibited'; and 'She does not allow me to touch her'. It gradually dawned on the social workers that this aspect had to be probed and brought out into the open if they were to understand one of the central sources of pain and violence in women's lives. Women usually explained their difficulty through statements such as: 'He is a drunk and wants sex at all times, even in front of the children'; 'He wants sex when I am sleepy and exhausted'; 'There is only one room where we all sleep'; and 'It makes a noise, letting everyone know what we are doing'. Older women—often mothers-in-law—were adept at limiting interaction between newlywed couples, preventing any closeness from developing between them. 'His mother wakes up and sits on the threshold after opening the door' was a comment that more or less summed up the situation.

Then there were cases where women complained about sexual violence in their marriages, along with what they considered sexual 'misdemeanours'. This included the use of pornography, being made to participate in masturbation, anal sex, and the like. Special Cell workers thus discovered what women's understanding of acceptable sexual behaviour in marriage was. Anything not known to them was bad or disrespectful of them as married, 'good' women, implying that only 'bad' women, or prostitutes, could be expected to do such things. There was little talk at the Special Cell of women's desires, pleasure, or their wants in sexual interactions. A large part of the narratives derived from what women understood to be socially or culturally sanctioned sexual behaviour. As the women had come to the Special Cell for help to resolve their immediate problems, they felt they had to convey their thoughts and feelings in a socially acceptable form if they were to achieve their objective.

Manifestations of the 'self rerouted' could be seen on women's bodies, and in their physical and mental health. A large number of the women who came to us were thin, anaemic, and suffered from tuberculosis. Violence, both mental and physical, seemed to lower women's immunity, making them susceptible to diseases like tuberculosis, which was serious, given their dire economic and environmental conditions (Nagraj 1996). The women showed little interest in themselves and their bodies. They talked of being fed up, listless, and feeling tired all the time. Tense all through the day, most of them were prone to anxiety, headaches, insomnia, and nightmares (Dave and Solanki 2000).

Reasons for Violence and Solutions

The main reasons for abuse, as perceived by the women, were unfulfilled promises of dowry, alcoholism, and infidelity of the spouse. The problems uncovered in the course of the Special Cell's interventions included physical violence, mental harassment, depriving women of a dwelling, and desertion. Research studies show that women approach an external agency for help after their immediate family, relatives and community have been unable to assist them in leading lives free of violence. They go to the police when a violent precipitating event occurs that threatens their life, the life of their foetus or child, or their marriage (Dave and Solanki 2000). My contention is that there are two more reasons, independent but interconnected, for women seeking support: one, women believe in relationships and webs of relationships (Gilligan 1982); and two, women are socialised to believe in relationships—to maintain and nurture them—more so when it comes to marriage and the family.

Women who came to the Special Cell were trying to find ways to keep alive relationships that gave them access to resources now denied, including social status and economic sustenance. They approached us in the police office because they saw the state as having the power to stop violence and restore normality. Relationships of all kinds depend on the social, cultural and political milieu a person is in. Each class, caste and sub-caste has intricate rules for social and economic relationships. It is these that make for women's socialisation and experience, which govern their beliefs and values. All these played pivotal roles in their quest for a non-violent solution to their marital problems.

The abused women were aware that they were not treated with dignity, and were not highly valued in the family or the community. They had grown up knowing that women were vulnerable to being harassed and perceived as sexual beings above all. Many had experienced violence in their natal homes, or had observed or known of it in their extended family and community. They had thus been trained to sidestep circumstances that could lead to violence. Norms, rituals, practices, and experience had taught them to view themselves as existing within fenced enclosures. In spite of this elaborate social design, they came to the Special Cell to complain about violence.

To put it in simple terms, most of the women who approached us saw themselves as human beings who wanted to live in harmony with their spouses, and they were ready to struggle for it. Women intuitively strive for personhood and agency in their battle against violence. To my mind, it is this spirit that yearns for well-being that guides them to places like the Special Cell. Many women who sought our help wanted to stay in their marriages and relationships, but wanted them to be non-violent. Historically, most of the mechanisms to mitigate difficulties in marriages—figuring the family, community leaders, or the law—did not negotiate for non-violence. Strife, aggression, and even cruelty were not perceived as violence or a crime, especially because marriage and the family were in the realm of the private.

The Special Cell viewed abused women's desire to live in a non-violent home as a non-negotiable demand. It was to be upheld, nurtured and struggled for. This belief was iterated in all conversations, communications and negotiations. We did espouse respect for the aggressor as a value, even though it was sometimes difficult to practise. This principle led us to ask women what kind of marriage and relationship they wanted to achieve with the Special Cell's intervention. The simple answer was, 'Let him stop beating me.' Women's tolerance to violence had almost ended by the time they arrived at the Special Cell. More often than not, there was some other factor that added to this, emboldening them and making them see it as an opportune time to get help from the outside. These other factors included grown-up children who had begun earning, sons old enough to defend their mothers, support from the natal home, husbands not having an income, and wives having to make money to look after the family.

Table 2.4: Emotional State of Violated Women at the Time of Approaching the Special Cell

Sr. No.	Emotional state of the violated women at the time of approaching Special Cell	N=303	Percentage
1	Confused	183	60.4
2	Upset	166	54.8
3	Angry	88	29.0
4	Sad	79	26.1
5	Trapped	66	21.8
6	Feeling not trusted	47	15.5
7	In pain	38	12.5
8	Guilty	9	3.0
9	Revengeful	41	13.5
10	Helpless	168	55.4
11	Suicidal	57	18.8
12	Tension	209	69.0
13	Stressed/Pressured	113	37.3
14	Hopeful	187	61.7
15	Clipped story-brief	10	3.3
16	Feeling trapped in roles	19	6.3
17	Determined to confront violence	59	19.5
18	Fearful	173	57.1
19	Apprehensive	80	26.4
20	Any Other	20	6.6

Source: Apte 2004.

The Special Cell saw a pattern in the flow of women, which was governed by the weather, festivals, and school examinations and holidays, but there was a steady stream of them at all times. Everyone wanted to rebuild relationships that did not include violence, which meant that they would have to be based on trust, faith and mutuality. Our emphasis during negotiations for reconciliation was on non-violence, even if some other reasons for discord were set aside. For this was the only way that women could regain some part of their agency and autonomy—in other words, a say in their own lives. An evaluation study of the Special Cell conducted by an independent consultant in 2004 gave us ample data to understand the changes that women underwent, their perceptions about the process, and the gradual re-emergence of a stronger self.

Table 2.5: Impact of Special Cell Intervention on the Woman's Feelings

Sr. No.	Impact of Special Cell intervention on the woman's feelings	N=303	Percentage
1	I was heard/listened to sincerely	298	98.3
2	I felt she/he understood my problem	285	94.1
3	She/he believed me	193	63.7
4	Got confidence to solve my problem	188	62
5	Was given respect	159	52.5
6	Was given time and ear	280	92.4
7	Felt emotionally understood/light	228	75.2
8	Felt like coming back to the cell	188	62
9	Any Other	19	6.3

Source: Apte 2004.

The data shows that women articulated a set of complaints at the first meeting, but that more details emerged with further interaction. What was initially stated was often a one-dimensional problem; however, this soon acquired a multidimensional character, edifying both the women and the Special Cell workers, and changing the course of intervention. As the women began critically examining their situation in the company of social workers, they gained a new perspective and saw what they would like as a solution. They also learnt to identify trends and patterns in their lives, and thought of the interventions that were required to change its course.

Table 2.6: What did she Learn from her Interaction with the Special Cell Worker?

Sr. No.	Learnt from her interaction with the Special Cell Worker	N=303	Percentage
1	Clarity of the problem	147	48.5
2	Importance of papers/documents	22	7.3
3	Importance of self/self-expression beyond roles	21	6.9
4	Importance of taking decisions for oneself	72	23.8
5	Violence need not be accepted	34	11.2
6	Violence is a crime	55	18.2
7	That it's not my fault	39	12.9
8	Even husband cannot violate me	34	11.2
9	Information and alternative options	222	73.3
10	Any other	5	1.7

Source: Apte 2004.

Figure 2.1, based on the responses of the women who came to the Special Cell, displays the emotional changes that took place in them following intervention.

Figure 2.1: Emotional Changes in Women after Intervention

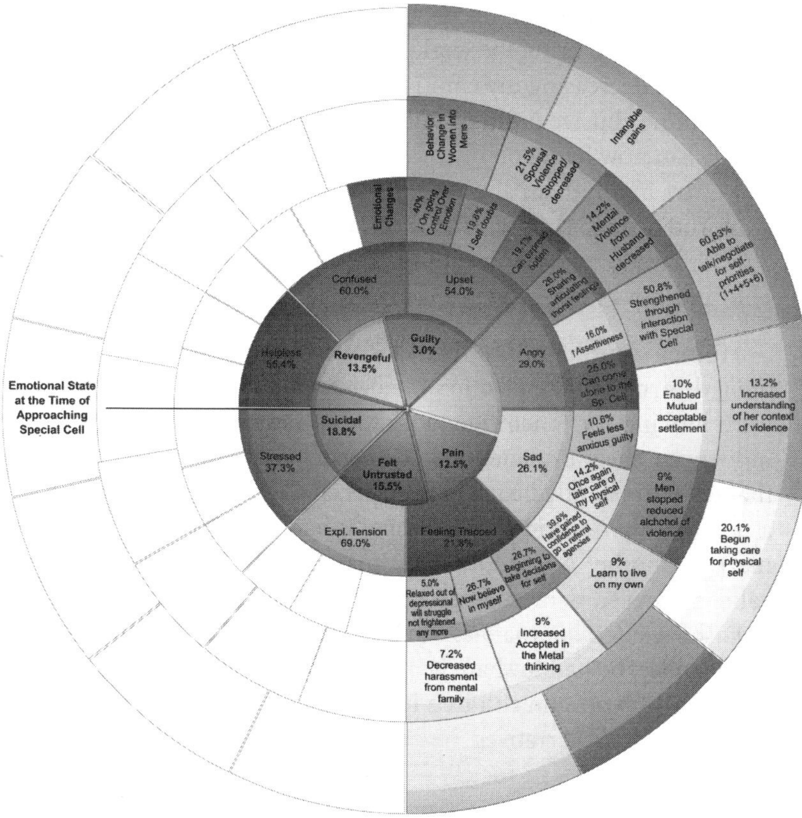

Source: Dave 2013.

Snapshots that Tell Stories

Here are a few quotes from women on the welcome changes that occurred in their lives after the Special Cell gave them a hand, and what it meant to them in a larger social context.

- 'I moved away from my abusive partner. Although I tried to get help to bond with him, the change did not occur.'
- 'I have modified my expectations. Instead of living in an abusive marriage, I am divorcing my husband.'
- 'I am changing roles. From just being someone who takes care of the children, I am seeking joint custody of them.

But my husband will still have the primary responsibility of providing for us.'

- 'I am re-entering the workplace.'
- 'I am decreasing my emotional engagement and dependence on my abusive partner.'
- 'I am now living on my own.'
- 'You live with an abusive partner, or you live alone, or away. You have to choose what is acceptable and happier for you.'
- 'I have to take responsibility for myself. Once you are alone, you have to take care of yourself.'

Women were defined by their class, caste and community, which often determined the position they were in and the solutions they were looking for. Their age, education, and work status further influenced their expectations. This gave rise to some demands that were frequently heard in the Special Cell. If the husband had a relationship outside the marriage, it had to stop, and if he had married another woman, the first marriage had to be considered valid. However, if the person complaining was the second wife, then she wanted her marriage to be acknowledged. If the husband had a house, he had to share it, and provide what was necessary to maintain his wife and children in reasonable comfort.

The women's narratives, heard by Special Cell workers, clearly showed their status in society as dependants, with no control over their lives and resources. Often helpless, they were compelled to accept crumbs and be reconciled to being the lesser partner. They were also so role-bound that the process of getting them to think critically was painful, as was persuading them to accept reality. Long-held beliefs had been taken for granted, and never questioned. It was disorienting when these were shaken. Very few of the women who came to the Special Cell were on friendly terms with their husbands. The starkness of Friedrich Engels' definition of marriage and family as a 'consolidation of sexual and economic activities' was manifest in a majority of the cases the Special Cell dealt with.

I recollect a few instances during my seven years of direct practice where the bonds between man and woman were role-governed, but not role-bound. Shades of this were observed occasionally in other cases as well.

One of the women liked her husband as a person, enjoyed sexual relations with him, and was happy sharing her life with him till he became an alcoholic and an abuser, the two feeding off each other. Even as they sat in the Special Cell office, negotiating the terms for reconciliation, they stole glances at each other, and accepted each other's demands without any serious arguments or caveats. The two evidently shared an emotional bond, although it had been disturbed. Accepting his behaviour had been the main problem, but he was ready to seek treatment for alcoholism.

A 27-year-old woman with a long scar on her cheek wanted the Special Cell to stop her partner, a pickpocket and chain snatcher, from abusing her. Her intention was to get us to use the police to indirectly threaten him. Neither wanted to stop living with the other. He said, '*Mohabat ki hai, haan*. I have loved her, I am not going to leave. Let her go if she wants to.'

A husband and wife, living in the same house at the time a complaint was made, met at the Special Cell for arbitration and to negotiate a compromise. The discussion aside, what they did was flirt with each other—communicating their feelings in a 'safe place'.

Dowry and its Aftermath

The lives of the women visiting the Special Cell revolved around their marriages and families, and these seemed to define their destiny. A traditional marriage is as much a celebration as it is about regulations and norms that standardise activities and behaviours. One such activity is the giving and taking of gifts to express happiness. Giving and receiving a dowry, a bad word today, is a practice that falls under this category, and it is a part of almost all marriages. Many of the women we met considered fulfilling this requirement a ticket to marital bliss. They often referred to marriages as 'settling the deal', or said, 'In spite of our difficulties, we did all that they expected—a marriage hall that had status, 300 guests, gold for the in-laws, and household articles for the new couple.' These weddings were always beyond the means of the bride's family. The women were aware of their family's economic position and the means by which funds had been raised for their weddings. But they saw it as the norm, more so because they would not get a share of their natal family's property. They also viewed a dowry as an investment in their future happiness. So weddings took place when the 'deal' was acceptable to both families, and the *kurbur* (dowry) was an integral part of the process.

Domestic violence arising from quarrels over dowry was a problematic issue. As defined by the law, a dowry is a payment given 'as consideration for the marriage', or as a precondition to it. But abuse was often the result when a woman's family failed to function as a consistent economic resource for the husband and his family. Women expected economic support and warmth in marriages, in return for the emotional care, nurture and sexual interaction they provided. They felt cheated when they believed that their part of the deal—giving a dowry—had been fulfilled, and yet their husbands insisted on getting still more from their families and subjected them to violence over it. Despite this, women continued to hope that their value as persons would be acknowledged by their marital families. This day-to-day living with the hope of better times made them cling to the known for their emotional and economic survival.

It is not poverty that is responsible for violence against women. When socially defined expectations of economic support from a wife's family are unfulfilled, it fuels anger and frustration in the husband. The easiest thing for him to do is turn on the 'reason', his wife, who he knows is vulnerable, dependent on him, and not very highly valued in society (Wyatt 2011). Dowry deaths continue to occur, the reasons for them are researched, legal remedies are sought, punishments are meted out, and society and women continue to celebrate marriages with exchanges of gifts. There were 8,383 dowry deaths in 2009 and 8,391 dowry deaths in 2010 (Crime in India Report 2011). A few parents and family members have come to the Special Cell with requests to investigate their daughter's or relative's death. Most of them knew these women had led troubled lives, but they did not see it as anything unusual, for that is what society's norms had led them to believe.

Closing Remarks

Another set of violated women who approached the Special Cell were lesbians facing family violence. It was often organisations and groups that approached us to get the police to intervene when women were held captive by their families. Restricting their mobility and confining them against their will were, according to the law, unlawful detention. Special Cells across Maharashtra have intervened in such cases, even though their number has not been high.

Most of the women who came to the Special Cell were accompanied either by their relatives, friends, or well-wishers. Enquiring about their relationship with those accompanying them helped us to gauge the extent of their social networks and the support they had. It was very reassuring when some of them introduced us to their mothers-in-law because it showed that women were not women's worst enemies, as patriarchy holds. Women who come to the Special Cell want to live, and live well. They have not lost faith in themselves yet, and require help to rebuild relationships based on trust.

3

Taking Root: Eliciting Police and State Response

Learning about the Police

The launch of the Special Cell was the beginning of an unplanned journey. With the police and social workers working together for the first time, we had to engage with a new set-up and evolve practices that would suit both us and them. It was imperative that we understood the police system, which was to aid us in our work on violence against women. So we set out to learn from every interaction with the police.

DCP (HQ) T. Singarvel, the nodal officer at police headquarters, was in charge of the official orientation. He took us around, showing us the control room, the nerve centre of police operations, the administrative offices, and the library. In the first three months, we visited every police station in the city. On our request, information about our visits was transmitted by the control room over the wireless, leaving police stations to draw their own conclusions on who was visiting and why. When we arrived at some police stations, we were told to come back later because the senior inspector was expecting some 'dignitaries', only to then find out that we were the luminaries. The idea of 'non-police' people being allowed to use police infrastructure to deal with violence against women was alien to the police. After a show of politeness—since we were the 'CP's guests'—each police station gave us an overview of crimes in its area, the kind of problems that women came to it with, and the police's opinion on them. It did not take us long to realise that the police's legal and constitutional roles were contested by their social role, which was tied to patriarchal values of patronage and control.

We sat with the CP every afternoon when he met the public. He thought that it would be educative for us, and also enable him to refer cases to us for immediate attention. Mr Ribeiro was an expansive person, who enthusiastically took on the roles of educator and mentor. He also sought our opinion on the police system as we saw it. While we may have been naïve, this gave us an opportunity to share our observations and concerns with him. For instance, when we visited the Bhoiwada police lockup, the stench of urine and vomit was very apparent, despite it having been washed for our visit. We happened to mention this to the CP, who enquired with the senior officers concerned. They explained that the quality of the food provided was poor because of budget constraints. We were later informed that a request seeking an increase in the budget had been sent to the government.

On our visit to the Dadar police station, we saw a young girl, who had been accused of stealing a gold necklace from her employer, being beaten by the police. The police had no business—legal or otherwise—beating a child to force a confession, and we brought this to the CP's attention. At another time, during a discussion with the CP, we inadvertently told him that a unit had only an officer who was 'holding charge'. The CP soon ensured that an officer was put in charge of the unit, which meant that the one holding charge lost his temporary position as its head. This was brought to our notice by the officer concerned, who happened to be the same person who had, in our first meeting with the CP, insisted that the Special Cell be accommodated in a separate office.

The afternoons also gave us a glimpse into the variety of people who came to the CP and the problems they brought with them, which were often complicated by class and gender. Some of the requests were pretty unreasonable, but since they mattered to the people making them, the CP tried to work his way around them. A sadhu wanted to take his cows from Mumbai to north India without hindrance from the police. He wanted a letter from the CP, allowing his cows free movement. Another man wanted to pray for Mr Ribeiro, but it had to be done in the CP's office. He was allowed to sit there and pray. An old woman complained of a noisy crow that always sat outside her window. She wanted the CP to put a stop to this nuisance. Another woman felt that her landlord had stopped her water supply, and wanted the CP to look into it. Although this came under the Essential Services Act, he referred it to us, with a request to pay a visit to the people involved.

Watching Mr Ribeiro, the person and the CP, in action, and the manner in which he dealt with a variety of issues and people was in itself an education. I always saw him dealing with people with warmth and concern, using humour to dissolve tension. He would listen to people, asking questions about the details to show them they had his attention. His attempt was to reassure people that both he and the police were interested in them, and that he was willing to take fair action. While hearing complaints from the public, he would at times pick up the phone and boom into it, saying that he wanted a report in a given period of time, or that he would like to speak to an officer. This invariably reassured the complainants, making them feel that they were being taken seriously and that they mattered.

A few months into our work, we were at the control room one evening, discussing our plans for home visits with the officer in-charge. The phone rang and he answered it. He then stood up, repeatedly saying 'Yes sir' into the phone. Hanging up, he said, 'That was the CP, wanting me to find out from the Andheri police station about a complaint made by the person in his chambers now.' That was when we discovered that those booming calls from the CP's room were made to the control room, which in turn relayed the message to the police stations or officers concerned. The CP did not call officers directly, overwhelming or intimidating them. His method of using the chain of command gave officers enough time to gather information and report back. The CP also took care of his men, while trying to satisfy the public. To many, he responded, 'I do not have supernatural powers, I am only a policeman.' To others, he said, 'This is not a police state, we have a democracy.'

Attending the police durbar in the CP's office on Fridays gave us another opportunity to learn about the police system, the people within it, and their community. Here, one saw what affected constables and inspectors and their families, and the impact of policing on their lives. Individual policemen brought their grievances, requests and anxieties to the durbar. Their concerns had to do with transfers, postings, housing problems, suspensions,

pensions, widows, and children's education. Policemen could present their case verbally or give in a written application. The issues handled were by and large serious, but there were a few eccentric ones as well. For example, an older constable requested that he be allowed to grow a beard (beards are not allowed, except for religious reasons). The CP asked, 'What happens if you do not grow a beard?' The constable answered, '*Dokya var parinam hoto*' (It affects my head and mind). The CP looked at him and said, 'Okay, go and grow a beard.' In an aside to us, he said, 'How am I supposed to protect the city with such policemen?'

We gradually realised that many of the policemen's families lived in squalor and poverty. Dysfunctional or disorganised families, family violence, and delinquent children were often their realities. Family housing was a long-term dream, and many constables lived in the city's slums. The sons of dead policemen were recruited to the police force to ensure that their families did not suffer, but this denied them a chance to choose a career. The stress of policemen's work adversely affected their families and personal relationships. We saw that policemen faced many health hazards, yet medical cover from their employer—the state—was minimal. It was augmented by the police welfare fund, which was raised from amongst themselves. Alcoholism and absenteeism were high, and the mental health of many policemen was at risk. The police saw and interacted day in and day out with the seamier side of life—a dehumanising process, if ever there was one.

Once, while waiting for help in a case at a police station, we witnessed a rather typical day in a policeman's work. A large number of people with various problems were talking to the station house officer (SHO), other officers, and constables. Meanwhile, the SHO got a call informing him of a riot at the police station's limits. He quickly informed his seniors, gathered a team of constables, hollered for a jeep, put on his holster, and telling us to wait, left the police station. He returned 30 minutes later, removed his holster, and got back to dealing with the waiting people. Then one of the constables, pointing to a group of people, told him that the 'other party' had arrived. The SHO immediately began reprimanding them. The group looked bewildered and a little scared. The constable realised he had made a mistake and tactfully pointed this out to the SHO, who fixed his stare on another set of people that was pointed out and, without a pause, began berating them.

Even though constables wielded a certain amount of power over the public, the hierarchical structure of the police force saw them quake if an officer upbraided them. An understanding of what command and control meant in different circumstances gradually dawned on us. In the police system, position and importance were communicated in a number of ways. Examples of this were the conventions to do with where the most important person would sit in a police car, or where he would sit if he was visiting a police station. As our familiarity with the police community grew, cases concerning policemen themselves were referred to the Special Cell by both officers and men. We knew the police were governed by rules and norms different from those governing ordinary citizens, and we created a separate intake register for them. This ensured that 'insider data' remained confidential. The network of help for these women came mainly from within the system—it was all kept within the family, so to speak. The Special Cell largely got cases involving the ill-treatment of policemen's wives, and the abuse of women police officers and constables in their homes or the workplace. However, not many instances of domestic violence among the women police were reported. This seemed to have to do with their self-respect and dignity—they probably felt humiliated at the thought of bringing this problem to social workers in the police office.

We participated in the police's Diwali *mela*, which was meant to celebrate the festival as a community and also to raise funds, and this brought us in touch with many more in the force. We were asked to man the lucky draw stall because they believed we would be honest and not pilfer the gifts—sort of protecting the protectors from the protectors. In the early days, we came across many such ironic situations. There was also a high degree of distrust among people within the police community, perhaps because distrust and suspicion were a part and parcel of their training and work. A teacher, Dr N. A. Gokarn, told me:

> Social work is built on the premise of faith and trust in human beings; the police have to begin with suspicion. These are two ends that have to work together towards similar goals, and there is bound to be a struggle.

While on visits to police stations and homes, we discovered parts of Mumbai that we knew nothing about earlier. For instance, a large tract of land on the southern coast belongs to the Mumbai Port Trust, where it has docks and internal roads. Driving through this area can cut the travel time to north Mumbai by half. Police cars could zip through these roads, which were not accessible to ordinary citizens. The police drivers knew many other routes that were shorter, and avoided the heavy traffic on the main roads. Soon, our reference point for home visits was the nearest police station, where we could obtain directions to reach our destination. That a third-generation Mumbai-ite like me could discover new areas in the city through the police was fascinating.

A Special Cell in Dadar

In 1988, Mr V. K. Saraf was the CP, and the Special Cell had completed four years of work. We had conducted training programmes for the Juvenile Aid Police Unit and for sub-inspectors and inspectors in the city's police stations, initiated Project Help, and provided resource persons for programmes on violence against women organised by community-based organisations, NGOs and educational institutions. The Special Cell was also drawn on by policemen of all ranks for a variety of reasons, its opinion was sought in cases of violence against women, and its help was sought when women had to be interviewed on sexual matters, or when academic information or research data was required by the police. Referrals to the Special Cell were on the rise, and women were coming to it from even the city's fringes.

The first four years of the Special Cell clearly demonstrated the potential of the strategic alliance with the police, and defined our area of work. Mr Ribeiro's letter of acceptance to our project proposal had granted the Special Cell three years (see Appendix 2). In the fourth year, a discussion with the CP enabled us to not only continue our work, but also expand it. This was a defining stage in the development of the Special Cell, a validation of its approach, and a recognition of its services in the battle on violence against women. The expansion came about when Professor Apte thought that we needed to make our services more accessible to women. Dadar seemed a good mid-point of the city at that time. We approached the CP and asked if it was possible to start a second Special Cell. Mr Saraf welcomed the idea, and added to our proposal by suggesting that it be in the police station. His reasoning was that being a separate unit would not enable the Special Cell to interact directly with the police. He also hoped that an association with the Special Cell would 'humanise' the police. The Dadar Special Cell began its work in 1988.

The women's movement and women's organisations were at the time vociferous in their demand that the police and the state address the issue of violence against women, including dowry harassment and deaths, and domestic violence. In 1983, the Delhi police set up a Crime against Women Cell (CAWC), manned by the police, to investigate cases of violence against women. In 1985, the first all-women police station was opened in Bhopal (Chikarmane 1999). To enable these initiatives, the police carved out units from existing personnel and resources, which, although laudable, was not wholly adequate. The CAWC's objectives were to ensure effective implementation of Section 498A of the IPC, which disallows husbands or their relatives from subjecting women to cruelty, and working to get rid of the psychological fear and hesitation that women had in reporting instances of abuse to the police.

Women's organisations and political activists in Mumbai also demanded a special effort from the police. The political ideologies of some of the organisations coloured the nature of their demands, and immediate action with inbuilt justice was expected, which translated into the police arresting the accused. The upshot was that what began as organisations using the help of constables and the law to obtain speedy justice was soon construed by women and their families as the police 'criminalising family relations'. This ultimately necessitated canvassing the help of women anew when it came to the campaign for the Protection of Women from Domestic Violence Act, 2005.

At around this time, the police would say, 'We put the man in the lockup, detained him, and the next morning she comes with a *toshadan* (tiffin) for him'; or 'If we put him in the lockup, she says, "Leave him after a few hours, he needs to earn. How will I feed my children?'" Or, 'Women need violence to stop and require temporary help. Marriages include strife and violence, and our arrest of the man poses a threat to her marriage.' In brief, women wanted arrests only to restrain their husbands from hurting them; however, they did not want those arrests to threaten their marriages.

The expectations of women's organisations fell within the realms of the legal and the extra-legal. They primarily wanted to help women use the power of the law and the authority of the police to counter violence and abuse. Their comprehension of justice involved a quick response and action to stop the abuse. For instance, a woman had an abortion, and this was followed by the man she was engaged to backing out of the relationship. A women's organisation understood this as violence against her. It insisted that they stay engaged, because the man had been responsible for the woman's pregnancy. That an engagement was essentially a trial period was lost in the sound and fury. The Special Cell increasingly understood what its strengths were, while recognising the difficulties and obstacles in its path, especially those of attitude and perception.

One-third of the women who approached the Special Cell had already been to the police. The violence and strife had continued, though, and they now wanted the help of social workers to stop it. The remedies found by the police were sometimes effective in the short term, but the problems recurred.

Table 3.1: Women's Expectations of the Police

Sr. No.	Assistance from police expected	N=303	Percentage
1	Quick Justice	11	3.6
2	Pressure to stop violence/Protection from abuser	26	8.6
3	Register FIR	13	4.3
4	Prosecution	8	2.6
5	Rectify police inaction	2	0.7
6	Register NC	44	14.5
7	Follow up Investigation/Inquiry	11	3.6
8	Executing orders of the Court	12	4
9	Any other	6	2

The women's movement wanted a special unit of the police to be formed to tackle violence against women, with personnel skilled in dealing with the issue. Increased interaction with the criminal justice system and engagement with the issue had led them to discover the high barriers that existed between women and justice. The law itself is based on the socio-political reality of women. The police are a large force, with more than 40,000 men and women on its rolls in the city of Mumbai alone. While the top brass has the sophistication to deal with a variety of issues and people, the shrewdness of policemen on the ground comes from their experience of dealing directly with multiple social realities. Individual perceptions and attitudes frequently affect their actions. While the leader of the force exerts considerable influence, the overlap of violence, women and gender relations leaves each officer free to loosely interpret where a case stands in the legal framework, which itself is partial to male authority in the private sphere or family. This leads to conflict and constant tension between the police and women activists, whom constables often refer to as bra burners, family breakers, and unhappy and ugly single women or divorcees.

The conflict is rooted in ideological positions. While women's organisations challenge power, authority and male supremacy, the police as an organisation embodies and upholds patriarchal rules, beliefs and practices. Yet this is the agency that wields the power of the state round the clock, and is the state agency for protection from violence. Women, who were brought into the force only to assist other women, constitute only about 2 per cent of the police in each state. Until 1971, women were not taken into the IPS, even if they passed the entrance exam. Recruitment to the police is not an open process in a majority of the states, and the number of women inducted depends on the limited number of posts available for them.

People believe in the rule of law in a democracy. However, they also encounter laws that do not seem to respect women or address them as equal citizens. This is because laws are also based on social and cultural assumptions on the value of women. While the Constitution advocates sexual equality and affirmative action for women and other disadvantaged groups, it is institutions, civil society organisations, and civil movements that have to dedicate time and resources to convert this into reality. The women's movement has to be a civil rights movement that addresses both individuals and systems, and aims to make women realise their value and status as unique individuals.

Each measure for social change requires close examination before it can be planned and delivered. Since all this is governed by the law and the final authority is the criminal justice system, women's groups end up using the law to change the law when there is a conflict. This relentless battle with the state and society for equal rights for women in the family and community has thrown up new challenges, and served as a source of learning. Every intervention adds to conceptual clarity, and enlarges the thinking and understanding of the women's movement, while contributing to a sceptical attitude vis-à-vis the state and the powerful in society.

In India, the law has at times been used to bring about desirable social change. The women's movement looks to the law and the police to respond to violence against women because that is the 'strong' arm of the state and the criminal justice system, and the only agency that can take immediate action. At the same time, it recognises that the police are often not very effective in getting violence to cease, and that their intervention could even lead to further victimisation; for policemen do not consider intra-familial and interpersonal assaults on women to be crimes. Their perceptions are influenced by deeply entrenched beliefs about the sanctity of the family, the superiority of the male, and the forbearance of women—the family as a unit has to be preserved at all costs. The reluctance of the police to intervene in familial violence amounts to a legitimisation of the use of violence as a form of social control (Chikarmane 1999). So what emerges is that women require a more nuanced and disaggregated kind of help than that offered by the police.

Emergence of the Socio-legal

Placing social workers within the premises of a police office to work with policemen on violence against women is a recognition of the need for social analysis in crimes against women. Although necessary, the law in itself is insufficient to address women's problems, and social change requires multiple strategies. In the case of the Special Cell, this developed into socio-legal work—a combination of social analysis and social work interventions informed by a feminist analysis of society, women and the law.

For the Special Cell, this was a slow process. We took many positions in the early days, but not necessarily with the clear objective of doing socio-legal work. Working with the police in a strategic alliance was instrumental in evolving a socio-legal mechanism to address violence against women. At the risk of repeating myself, I outline the factors that operated in favour of this.

- The Special Cell, located in a police office, could be approached by distressed women looking for assistance.
- It could intervene in both cognisable and non-cognisable offences, in accordance with women's needs.
- Women could approach the Special Cell directly, or be referred by the police.
- The Special Cell did not have an area of jurisdiction, unlike the police.
- Protection from violence was a state subject, and the police had an important role to play because the issues addressed were not limited to marital problems.
- The Special Cell's services supplemented and complemented the police's work. It was not a substitute for the police; rather, the two had considerable combined strength.
- The Special Cell did not only see all problems as individual ones, but also analysed them in terms of society, its institutions and systems.
- The Special Cell had men and women social workers to handle cases that required attention to details, and involved process-oriented work for problem-solving and rebuilding the violated women's dignity and self-respect.
- The Special Cell's trained social workers maintained a distinct identity in the police system.
- Conscious of the complex role the police had, the Special Cell worked within the framework of violence against women, the Constitution and human rights.

To begin with, the objectives of the Special Cell were:

- To review the complaints received and processed by the Social Service Branch.
- To offer immediate services, such as counselling, referrals for medical, psychiatric, educational and vocational help, police assistance, admission to institutions such as shelters, and legal aid.
- To be a liaison between the police and organisations for women and children.
- To create a critical awareness among women, professional groups and the general public about the atrocities committed on women and children.
- To document the work for critical review, and to develop material for policymakers and training programmes on violence against women, specifically for social workers and police personnel.

In 1999, we recognised that our work had included rebuilding the self-esteem, self-worth and dignity of abused women, and this was also included as an objective of the Special Cell. The second objective essentially refers to direct work with women, while the rest also have to do with society and institutions. All this guided our own training, and the way we handled our work. But what really steered the work to a large extent were the abused women's expectations, their belief in the right to life, their anticipation of state support to protect and sustain them and their children, and what we learnt from their social and material realities.

The database of the first 20 years shows us that as many as 53 per cent of the women who came to the Special Cell complained of physical abuse, and 80 per cent of them reported mental abuse (Dave and Solanki 2000; Special Cells 1997). Grievous injuries had been suffered by 12 per cent, and nearly 12 per cent of the women had attempted suicide because of violence in their marriages. So more than two-thirds of the women had grounds for legal cases, if they wanted to take that route. Only a third of all the women who came to the Special Cell had sought intervention from the police, and this was mainly for non-cognisable offences. Approximately 5 per cent of the women had registered criminal cases, or had approached the court before arriving at the Special Cell. And yet most of these women wanted social answers to their situation. The use of legal tools was asked for in varying degrees and for various reasons, but mainly because they saw the law and the police as having the power to stop violence. What most of them wanted was a carrot and stick approach to using the law, and they mentioned wanting 'to talk it over' with their partner, or 'convincing him' to stop violence.

Their reasons for going easy on the use of the law were many. There was the fear of a backlash and the marriage ending, as also apprehensions about the heavy cost of litigation and the criminal justice system, which they did not know anything about. Some women were unsure of their long-term goals, and did not want to lose their livelihood. Others felt the law should only be a last resort as far as social traditions were concerned, and that good women did not drag their families to the police and the court. Many also believed that their image in the family and community would be tarnished if they sought legal remedies. Underlying these considerations was a conviction women had—that treating their aggressors humanely was in their interest.

One of the crucial components of the Special Cell's work was rebuilding a woman's sense of self-worth and self-respect to enable her to think for herself and make choices. The assumption was that she had had little opportunity to acquire any self-confidence; that her rights had been violated; and that she had very limited control over her life, all of which had contributed to the trouble she was in today. As she had taken an important step towards living without violence by approaching the Special Cell, it endeavoured to be a place where she would be provided with the critical faculties needed to develop a sense of her self.

Thus, bringing together a socio-political understanding of women's lives, and the legal rights available to them, were of vital importance to enable them to stand on their own feet and defend their rights as autonomous individuals. The precipitating factor bringing women to the Special Cell may have been an incident of violence, or a fear or threat of violence, but that was usually the tip of the iceberg. When they narrated their stories, many interwoven strands emerged, which showed that they led complex and complicated lives. For instance, a Muslim woman had to be assisted to stop domestic violence, which was her immediate problem. Then she required legal aid for a divorce and negotiations with her natal family to get a share of the parental property, as well as help to find a job to earn a livelihood.

The kinds of help that women who came to the Special Cell required fell largely into three categories—aid to prevent violence; legal and police intervention; and counselling for reconciliation (Apte 2004; Dave and Solanki 2000; Haryana 2010; Special Cells 1997). Many of them implied that legal or police help would benefit them. In the course of the interventions, they articulated a range of concerns, issues and problems that had to be addressed. The data on the nature of problems indicated that social reasons were at the bottom of most of them. The inference we drew was the need to tackle them from a socio-legal angle, thus addressing the individual, the social structure, and its institutions and systems.

More than 80 per cent of the cases the Special Cell takes on involve family violence. This requires skills to work with individuals and families, a capacity to analyse social situations, knowledge of the law, and access to the police and courts. The same is needed in cases to do with child sexual abuse, trafficking of women, minor girls in brothels, missing or runaway women, mentally ill women, and children affected by domestic violence. Some of the cases that drew on our work with abused women had to be pursued in the High Court, or with state government committees.

At the time, the responses to violence against women were mainly in the form of laws on the subject in the IPC and the CrPC, specifically Section 498A of the IPC prohibiting a husband or his relatives from subjecting a woman to cruelty, and Section 304B of the IPC, which disallows a husband from harassing his wife with the demand for dowry. It is still largely so. Of course, there are also legislations against child marriage, sati and child sexual abuse, and the Protection of Women from Domestic Violence Act, 2005. Services for women who have suffered violence are available from voluntary organisations, which can be categorised as autonomous women's organisations, feminist organisations, welfare organisations, shelter homes, and community-based organisations. State government initiatives and structures were, and still are, mainly within the police system and the judicial system. Apart from the law, the police system has vigilance committees, all-women police stations, crimes against women cells, family counselling centres, and Special Cells. In the judicial system, the structures that address violence against women are the family courts, special women's courts, legal aid cells, and lok adalats. The state social welfare system has a central social welfare board, family counselling centres, short-stay homes, and programmes to generate awareness.

The vigilance committees, consisting of prominent citizens at the taluk, district and state levels, meet once a month, their role being that of an interface between the police and the public. They also advise and assist with social intervention when women and their families face difficulties. The all-women police stations deal with cases of violence against women at the district and city levels, but do not have the jurisdiction to register cases and often suffer from a lack of resources. The family counselling centres in police stations adhere to the police ideology of treating the institution of the family as sacrosanct, which translates into encouraging reconciliation when trying to resolve family conflicts. The terms used—family, marital discord, distress, conflicts, and the like, but not violence or crime—betray their perspective on abused women. Counselling is always emphasised, often not addressing the other requirements that women may have. Since the focus is on the family, and not on individual women, even the issue of violence sometimes gets sidelined. Crimes against Women cells are essentially similar to all-women police stations, although different states have organised them differently.

Working with the Police System

I would like to critically reflect on the Special Cell's work with the police system, based on our experience of working with it on cases, training programmes, research projects, and a large number of other activities. All this went into understanding the police force, its perspectives and motives, and contributed to developing the Special Cell's strategy and the socio-legal services it provides. Working in or with any system requires comprehending its many parts if one is to function effectively. Being part of a system requires one to have a grasp on its beliefs, ideology, and its resources—material and intellectual—as well as participate in its activities. This is more so when one is a new entrant to a system with an approach that is diametrically opposite to what one believes in. Finding common denominators is that much more difficult, especially when both parties are going through rites of passage. As the police is a large and powerful authority, its actions were confident and benevolent. We, as social workers, had much more at stake, and had to establish ourselves as being pro-women by proving that we possessed the ideology and skills to work on violence against women.

The Special Cell's first and last stop was people—human beings. Everyone had to be treated with respect and dignity, and valued for their role in society. Our interactions with people in the police system had to be within the ambit of social work principles and ethics, even as we learnt from them. It is recognised today that no one discipline can fully explain all social phenomena, or address the problems within them. Therefore, multidisciplinary teams and inter-disciplinary research and discussion are the orders of the day. I would like to point to some of the features that I consider contributed to the Special Cell's nuanced partnership with the police.

Cases were referred to the Special Cell by the police—the CP, senior officers, police stations, officers and men around our office, and officers we met at training programmes. There was no one institutional mechanism by which women were referred to the Special Cell, and this kept our channels of communication open and flexible. It meant being visible, being part of a professional network, and maintaining cordial relations, while being an effective force for the welfare of women. This brought us invitations to attend police seminars, to testify before police reform missions, and nominations to police committees on violence against women. We also met visiting police officers from different states who were interested in social issues, particularly those to do with women. This increased our visibility and built our network as cases of violence against women continued to be referred to us.

We discovered that the police referred cases to the Special Cell for a number of reasons. One was that we social workers were supposed to be experts in counselling. Cases of family violence, or marital problems as the police saw them, were perceived to need counselling or 'good advice', so that the institutions of marriage and family remained intact. In other words, women had to be made conscious of their marital roles and responsibilities for the larger good of the family and community. Another reason was that social workers, who were the feminine aspect when juxtaposed with the masculine police, had the ability to listen patiently to women's accounts of emotional and physical violence. The police were essentially trained to deal with the physical and legal aspects of violence against women, and the assumption was that they did not have the 'soft' skills to properly deal with emotionally burdened women.

Cases were also referred to the Special Cell because the police wanted to draw on its strengths and skills, which did not exist in abundance in the police force. The police, who recognised social realities and the real position of abused women in society, were often ready to acknowledge that we had the skills and expertise to help out. Data from studies on the Special Cell shows that the police referred 20.01 per cent of the cases handled by it between 1984 and 1990 (Special Cells 1997), 13.1 per cent between 1990 and 1997 (Dave and Solanki 2000), and 24.8 per cent in 2003 (Apte 2004).

The police have often been accused of corruption and misuse of power, both by officers within it and the general public. This was reflected in their referrals to the Special Cell when 'good' women or their relatives were sent to it, to ensure that the victims would not be browbeaten by ordinary policemen. Women were also referred by policemen to the Special Cell when they suspected that their superiors or political leaders would use their power to influence cases to the detriment of the women. Yet another reason was that the police often believed that cases of domestic violence did not deserve their time and attention.

In 2003, the Deputy Inspector General of Police, Prevention of Atrocities on Women (DIG-PAW), made a presentation at a conference in Brazil on women and the police, which summarised why the police in Maharashtra had adopted the Special Cell model. According to this paper, the rationale for the police's strategic alliance with social workers was based on four factors.

- The police's felt need: Although the police were the first agency abused women approached, there was a mismatch between their needs and the services provided, which resulted in short-term responses that forced women to compromise.
- The police sub-culture: The police tended to accord a low priority to dealing with violence against women, seeing it as a soft sector, which led to disinterest and slow action.
- Lack of specialised training: The police had very limited counselling skills, especially to deal with trauma and family issues, and to give women the emotional sustenance they needed.
- Better than others: The police believed the Special Cell to be an adequate mechanism when compared to the efforts made by the Mahila Suraksha Samiti, grievance redressal cells for women, and all-women police stations.

The Special Cell received a few applications to look into women's deaths in its initial days. Upon inquiring, we often found that these had been copied to us, and that the people concerned had not visited the Special Cell. But in one such case, the parents of the woman came to the Special Cell, and we pursued the case. We met the DCP of the zone along with the parents, and he was cordial, having been introduced to us earlier in a meeting organised by the CP. He heard us out, and said he would look into the matter in a week's time. The following week, he explained that he had studied the file, and the investigation showed the woman had died because of accidental burns. It was not a suicide or murder, as suspected by her parents. To add weight to his argument, he called the investigation officer, who said that the woman had wailed and called out, 'Do not leave me and go', to her husband as she was being taken to the hospital. He emphasised that the relationship between the two was 'so good' that the woman had called for her husband even when she was in great pain. The assumption here was that if he had been responsible for burning her or trying to kill her, she would not have called him.

We discussed the case with the police and asked, 'Why was he leaving her if the relationship was so good, and why did she need to call out to him and ask him not to leave?' Thinking of an answer to this question made the police pause, and the DCP said that he would re-examine the file. We left, and the parents did not come to the Special Cell again. Much later, we met the DCP at a training programme, and he told us that the case had ended with the husband being convicted. There were many cases where Special Cell workers intervened, either to pose a question, or provide further information and share documents with the police. Cases of death at the Special Cell were few and far between, but we gave inputs in several criminal cases filed for violence against women under Sections 498A, 323/324, 504, 375, and 354 of the IPC, and under the Dowry Prohibition Act, 1961, and the Child Marriage Restraint Act, 1929.

Police Attitudes and Perceptions

Special Cell workers had to not only learn what police procedures and processes were, but also what police perceptions and attitudes were. This was in addition to knowing about women's responses to the law and the police, and the effect that criminal cases had on them and their families. Laws, which had at one time seemed powerful enough to stop violence against women, were diluted by social realities and the ways in which the criminal justice system operated. We also discovered that sections of the CrPC could be used to prevent domestic violence if the police became a complainant and registered a case on behalf of a victim. But the police saw domestic and family violence as marital problems. Rape, according to most of them, occurred because skimpily dressed women roamed the streets at night. I was told by many policemen that their training schools had skipped the section on rape, and that it had not been talked about or discussed. The explanation was that it was avoided because it was about women and sex, and that they were there to study about crime. The social and political repercussions of crimes against women were not always a part of policemen's thoughts or actions.

Although the growing debates on women's rights and gender justice were part of the day-to-day work of policemen, they were distant concepts to them. Their general perception of women was confined to the socially prescribed roles of mother, sister, wife, and daughter. They found it difficult to see women other than as persons who reproduced and nurtured, and rarely saw them as persons in their own right. A study of the non-cognisable offences register of one police station for a year showed that more than 32 per cent of the women who came to it had reported domestic violence, but that the police had done little except enter it in the register and advise them to go to court (Dave and Solanki 2000).

A hierarchical organisation with a command and control ethos and a strong patriarchal leaning, the police had a good understanding of other social hierarchies—of caste, class, gender, location, and so on. While the Special Cell operated within this environment, its specific role had to be separate when necessary. Policemen have to take an oath to be true to the Constitution and to play a role in keeping with it. In practice, however, these promises are under constant threat, with the power and authority of the police force representing both a challenge and a danger to the constitutional goal of equality. In reality, what constables promise to do is owe allegiance to their superiors. Caste, class and gender play oppressive roles within the police organisation, and among the people they serve. And while policemen frequently use or abuse their power for their own benefit, their superiors and political leaders are not far behind in treating them with cynicism.

We learnt in the early days of our work that law and order and VVIP duty topped the police agenda, and that crime came only second. Violence against women was largely categorised as a 'social act', and this did fall within the police's core work; however, they did not give it the attention it required (Dave and Dharmadhikari 1987). While the police understood the harshness of the caste system (33 per cent of them belonged to the lower castes, and had got jobs because of reservations), the same consideration was not forthcoming when it came to gender hierarchies and the subjection of women in society. Policemen's socialisation constructed women as soft, emotional entities who were meant to be men's companions, and this was deeply embedded in them. So intervening in marital or family issues played out in front of them was uncomfortable. Their private lives mirrored these beliefs.

We, as Special Cell workers, experienced differential treatment by the police due to our being TISS-educated women and men from the urban middle class, and our having been given a letter of authority by the CP, and police vehicles to travel in. Of course, the strongest factor was gender. In the initial years, we paid significant attention to the way we dressed and addressed the police. We also debated socio-political issues with them, wanting to be respected, and not treated as 'do-gooders' from classes that could afford it. At times, we downplayed our different abilities so as to not stand out as special—this was also a part of our effort to meld with the system.

Imbibing constitutional values has been difficult for a large section of the police force. Not all of them have experienced democracy in their lives, in their families, or in their communities. When criticised, the police often say, 'Policemen come from the same society', meaning that their social values are similar to those of the people who come to them. To them, the view that the police have to be 'above it' and uphold the constitutional values of equality, liberty and fraternity is not fully justified. The law is seen by most policemen as something with which to restrain or constrain social activities, human behaviour and relationships. In our experience, these views only varied marginally among police officers of different ranks.

Police investigations into the rape of girls between the ages of 12 and 18 were driven by the perception that they had been 'inviting' and 'enticing', which had led to 'love affairs'. The view was, 'If she was going out with boys, there was bound to be a sexual relationship, and it would have been with her consent', or 'Only when parental and societal pressures mount do girls cry rape'. Thus, their investigations were influenced by the beliefs they held. The police do not easily accept that a girlfriend has the right to say no, and that a man cannot force himself on her. They do not always comprehend that it is the act of violation, not the relationship, that has to be the focus of their attention. Our experience showed that these beliefs were strong across all levels of the police force.

In many forums, police officers have proudly announced that they have got a rapist to marry his victim, or that they are enforcing marriage, since in any case the woman's life has been 'ruined' and the best 'protective remedy' is to marry her off to the aggressor. In particular, if a child has been conceived in a rape, the rehabilitation is considered complete with marriage. The police have been largely unable to appreciate that by locking a victim with her aggressor in a social contract with legal blessings, they are further violating her, the law, and the Constitution. They explain that such marriages are the 'practical approach', and that they give women some justice, which they have no guarantee of getting if the process of the law takes its course. The police do not always propose legal answers to violence against women—their own faith in the system is often shaky.

In many discussions and debates, police officers have maintained that the law cannot bring about social change, and that it is society that has to change. They do not perceive that the law can be a vehicle of change, and uphold values and aspirations, especially if they suspect it is attempting to change unequal gender relations. This approach frequently leads to victims being victimised multiple times in their lives. While describing the present violence, several women who came to the Special Cell talked of having been raped when they were younger, the roles the police and other adults had played, and the emotional impact it had had on them (Purvin 2003). Making connections between what we heard and understood from women and the police was one of the keys to developing the socio-legal services of the Special Cell. This was aided by feminist thinking and analysis, research, and women's practical needs.

The emotional responses of policemen to social issues could best be explained by the fact that most of them live in relationships similar to the ones others of their class have, and that they all share the same belief system. Yet, it is these things that they need to question in their roles as policemen. They also have to take a second look at the coercive masculine power of the police if they are to effectively protect women from violence. On the other hand, policemen's profession demands that they remain emotionally distant. Emotion is a limited asset that is lost when one uses it. Offering sympathy means having less for yourself, which often leads policemen to alcohol and drug abuse (McElhinny 1995).

A senior police officer at a seminar once told me that his mother was not educated, but had brought up her children very well, which made it patently clear that women's education was 'not important'. This was an IPS officer from an upper-caste, middle-class family. His view was that the fact that his mother had no formal education could not devalue her, and he had a strong emotional bond with her. However, he made the mistake of generalising on the basis of this, paying no heed to the issue of why women as a category did not receive enough education. While I appreciated that his mother had to be valued in spite of not being educated, did this mean that the answer to a widespread social problem was to continue denying formal education to all women? This was my response, and adding to it, I suggested that he ask his mother if she would have liked to have had a formal education. Social analysis and new understandings were slow to be absorbed by the police when they were not backed by a memo, a government policy, or a law. If there was a law in place, they had mechanisms to ensure compliance. But self-directed growth from what they experienced and observed around them was slow.

Training Programmes

The organising and conducting of training programmes have given the Special Cell tremendous opportunities for learning. Formal and informal interactions with the police developed and sharpened our analytical skills, and improved our ways of working with them. The training programmes were a mutually enriching process because presenting our work and analyses to the police was always a challenge. While we went with well-prepared case studies, reading, and experiences of working with abused women, we were unable to match the police in the breadth of their experience—the years of work many of them had put in, the number of cases they had handled, and the broad spectrum of human behaviour they had encountered. We learnt over a period of time to present our views and analyses on violence against women in conceptual terms. It was not necessary to be descriptive, because they too had the experience. It was our analysis of this that was of the essence. This also had the potential to get through the defensive, or even aggressive, stances adopted by many of them in training sessions.

Some of the police officers tried to intimidate Special Cell workers, especially the women trainers. They used their knowledge of the law, their experience, and their sheer confidence at being police officers to overpower the arguments presented. Feedback, especially verbal and in small groups, revealed that the police trainees were better able to stomach unsettling gender analyses from trainers who were men. While women trainers were mainly seen as adversaries, they had some empathy with male resource persons, and there was presumably some kind of male bonding.

The training sessions provided an opportunity to Special Cell workers to convert their experience of working with abused women, the police system, and the criminal justice system into a database of sorts that could be used for education and communication. It prompted them to look at their experiences thematically, thereby building training resources. It also gave them an insight into their areas of interest, which led to further reading and research. Three areas that benefited from this were: analysing the violence against women; investigating child sexual abuse; and developing skills and strategies to communicate with abused women and children who had been affected by domestic violence. Special Cell workers built networks with the police through the training programmes, which gave them the opportunity to travel to districts in Maharashtra and to other states. They took a busman's holiday, taking a break from their daily work to add to their larger understanding of violence against women. They interacted with the police in different places and with local women's organisations working on the issue, while attempting to get an idea of the socio-political climate in which they were located.

The training programmes were also sites where different dynamics were played out. If high-ranking police officers were involved and the programme was well-organised, this told us that some importance was being attached to the subject, and this was reflected in the sessions. The programmes also allowed us to interact with multiple actors working on violence against women within the system, such as members of the police, the judiciary, the forensic department, the health system, and the district collector. We realised that pumping resources into systems was not enough, as it was individuals who brought dynamism, energy, conviction, and passion to the overall battle on violence against women. The design and implementation of the training programmes, and the participation of several stakeholders assisted us in building networks for coordination with different arms of the criminal justice system.

Social workers of the Special Cell learnt to navigate through the corridors of power and authority of the police organisation to arrange training programmes. Each programme required getting permission from an SP, picking suitable dates, coordinating with a nodal officer appointed by the SP, arranging a venue, training materials, and logistical support for the trainers and trainees, and seeking the cooperation of resource persons, like the IG of the police range, judges of the district court, prosecutors, or forensic officers. Explaining the objective of the programme needed clarity of purpose, and the Special Cell gained knowledge of the criminal justice system not only from case work, but also through education.

In every training programme, we met policemen of different ages and experience with diverse views and beliefs, which influenced their interpretation of the law. Their social position and gender also influenced the lenses through which they understood social phenomena. With the help of training methods—experiential learning, group exercises, and discussions and presentations—the police were asked to critically reflect on social and gender roles in the context of violence against women, and their role and responsibility as they saw them. In the process, they reviewed their policies and the procedures required by the law, and examined how they worked together towards the larger goal of justice.

That the constitutional provisions of equality and positive bias needed to be implemented in the police organisation was apparent. There were not enough policewomen to deal with women prisoners, and with women detained while on trial or after being charged with a crime. Even with only two or three policewomen in every police station, the required infrastructure (such as toilets, changing rooms and housing) was non-existent. Nor were there gender-aware policies for postings, transfers, promotions, and the like. This in turn was used to explain inefficiency and the ineffective handling of cases and situations. For many years, policewomen's training was of a shorter duration, and they learnt little of how to conduct investigations, the law, and handling arms (Chikarmane 1999; Chakravarty 1998).

Policewomen spoke of their fight for equality in day-to-day work, battling with a variety of prejudices, discouragement, limited opportunities, and sexual harassment. Their conflicting roles created difficulties in their social and personal lives. As policewomen, they were expected to be 'tough', but being women, they were placed in what were seen as undemanding sections of the police organisation, which were dominated by men who held firm to the tenets of patriarchy. At home, as traditional wives and daughters, their roles had to be reversed. They had a job that gave them a degree of power, but their status at work and at home was quite low.

We embarked on the training programmes with resources from the TISS, and before long began receiving assistance from the central government for district and region-level programmes. After the first two rounds of training in all the districts of Maharashtra, funds for training on violence against women were made available to the DGP. This allowed us to consistently interact with the police force in the state for 20 years or so, while orienting them on the main issue the Special Cell dealt with.

We also participated in national-level efforts to promote awareness on violence against women. For instance, we took part in a gender planning training project organised by the central government in collaboration with the British Council and the Institute of Development Studies, Sussex; conducted training programmes at the Lal Bahadur Shastri National Academy of Administration, Mussoorie; and were resource persons for the development of training modules for the Sardar Vallabhbhai Patel National Police Academy, Hyderabad, and the National Commission for Women, New Delhi. Based on the evaluation study of the Special Cell, the UN Fund for Women, New York, invited us to share methodological concerns in evaluation research on violence against women. We were also invited by police departments in Orissa, Madhya Pradesh, Haryana, and Delhi to conceive and conduct training programmes for their personnel. Being resource persons for different programmes organised by police schools and colleges was a regular feature of the work at the Special Cell.

Resistance to Outside Influence

A meaningful interaction took place in 1993–94, when representatives of TISS and the police formed part of a committee set up by the DGP to examine the issue of having a cadre of social workers in the criminal justice system. The department of criminology and correctional administration at TISS had initiated a field action project in 1990 called Prayas, which aimed to assist youth offenders and first-time offenders. This project grew out of years of steady work with the criminal justice system. Given the Special Cell's experience of effectively operating within the police system from the 'victim' end, TISS proposed that the police consider including social workers in their system. The committee was set up by the DGP in response to this.

This was the first time that we sat in a committee with the police, and what we heard were their reservations about including persons from a different sphere of activity in their organisation. The ideologies of the two sides differed, and the police keenly believed in the need to preserve their territorial rights and control their resources. They felt that each law to do with social reform had burdened them with larger responsibilities, and they were bent on strongly resisting any official policy that supported or welcomed a 'social science input'. Many of the officers had a deeply entrenched belief in the system. They were quick to advance arguments like: 'We too had ideals, but to survive, we needed to be practical and not aspire for the moon', which was a way of belittling our arguments as ideals that had little chance of becoming reality. Pragmatism was a recurring theme while working with the police. Having met young police trainees with strong ideals, or even a readiness for heroism, the question that worried me was what the system did to erase idealism and optimism.

The arguments for not including social workers in the police force were layered, with many interwoven strands. I attempt to point out what their main elements were. To begin with, 'outsiders' could not be allowed access to the complex police system, and they could not be trusted with its secrets. Needing support from the outside could also be construed as the police admitting that they were not doing an efficient job. We had heard these viewpoints right from the first meeting we had with Mr Ribeiro and police officers from the Social Service Branch (SSB) and the Juvenile Aid Police Unit (JAPU).

There was ambivalence in accepting the intervention of social workers while working with women, the poor and the downtrodden. The officers noted that social workers did what they could within what was patronisingly referred to as the 'doing good' framework, and that this could have a positive effect on the image of the police if they were situated within it. At the same time, they did not want social workers to utilise any police facilities or resources, which were perceived as limited (Apte 2004; BPP 1998). The police drew its authority and power from the Constitution and the law, and officers were unable to think of social workers within the same frame. They considered social work a benign occupation, but recognised that it could at times help individuals by doing more than just following the rules. Their vast experience of working with rules, laws and systems made them aware of the limitations these had.

I think it was their premise of social work that was faulty, not their aims. Social work was perceived as a 'soft sector', which was sensitive, emotional and caring. These things mattered in personal and private lives, but not in police stations, where the police did 'hard core work', adhering to logical and rational principles.

The police felt they were being given a role in enforcing an increasing number of social laws, which affected their efficiency. They did not think these laws had much to do with the prevention of violence and crime. Their job was to maintain law and order, and investigate crimes using their training and experience. The tools available to them were legal ones, and they believed this restricted their role in supervising social laws.

We experienced aggressive and belligerent behaviour in the meetings, alongside being treated in a very patronising manner. The TISS members had to repeatedly argue that multi-disciplinary work was required to address complex social realities, with many groups—such as women and Dalits—claiming that their rights be recognised. It was very difficult to communicate our conviction that change could be brought about from within the system to those who considered themselves 'insiders' of the system. We believed in harnessing the energy and knowledge within the system, the importance of socio-legal work, and using the law as a tool for social change in our hierarchical and oppressive social system, as the Constitution had envisaged. We were being spokespersons for the marginalised, while the police did not want to direct their resources to violence against women till it became a crime.

We attempted to be rational and logical, while also being pleasant and cordial, but it was a hard act to pull off. The TISS faculty balanced and supported each other's arguments. We were the ones who wanted to enter their system, and this forced us on the back foot. They did not want us to enter, but felt threatened, and this made them hostile, antagonistic and forceful. The process of trading arguments for and against a social work cadre in the criminal justice system went on for six months. Finally, the committee's report recommended that a social work cadre be formed, and pointed out the socio-legal parameters that could be adopted to give it shape. This was submitted to the DGP and the Department of Home in 1993. That was the last we all heard of it.

Persisting with the police system in Maharashtra on the issue of violence against women led to the work of the Special Cell becoming known to many in the police network all over the country. The joint commissioner of police in the Crime against Women Cell (CAWC) of the Delhi police contacted the department of social work at Jamia Millia Islamia in 2008 for help in counselling abused women. They brought the Special Cell model adopted by the Maharashtra police to his notice. He invited the Special Cell to make a presentation to his team, and was appreciative of its approach.

This was followed by sending seven officers of the Delhi police to Mumbai to study the functioning of the Special Cell. The joint commissioner also used the police network to check with senior police officers in the states where Special Cells had then been set up—Maharashtra, Haryana and Rajasthan—to convince himself of their utility. Once he received corroboration, he went all out to convince his superiors and find funds for the project. The Special Cell of the Delhi police began functioning in 2009, 25 years after the first CAWC in 1983.

The first 25 years saw the Special Cell surely but steadily evolve its own way of doing things, while working in tandem with the police. It consolidated its position in Maharashtra, and introduced the idea to Rajasthan, Haryana and Madhya Pradesh. The next five years saw five more states in the country adopt the Special Cell strategy.

Research Projects and Reports

In 1985, we were invited to be members of the Mahila Dakshata Samiti (MDS), a monitoring body at police stations mandated by the government of Maharashtra to review cases of violence against women. Since we were from TISS, the additional commissioner of police, Mr Arvind Inamdar, suggested that we undertake a study of police records to understand cases of dowry deaths, harassment and family violence registered under Section 498A of the IPC. This was the first instance of the police sharing data and records with the Special Cell for research.

In the course of our work, we found that the police's knowledge of law and procedure was phenomenal, although their convictions often coloured their investigations. The police department had a statistical wing, which maintained data and records, but systematic research and data analysis to improve functioning was not a serious goal. To us, learning on the job had meant imbibing lessons from the cases handled by the Special Cell and what we saw and heard, or drawing on the experience of senior police officers. Thus, the invitation to study police records in the early years of the Special Cell was very welcome. Every few years we found or met officers in different positions who were willing to open doors, and this not only provided us with very useful learning opportunities, but also affirmed our belief that change from within was a way to build democratic relationships.

The study that resulted, 'Shades of Courage', had data and case studies from 1988 to 1995, but it came into the public domain only in 1999. This was followed by the police granting us further permission to delve into their records. This led to three research projects, which produced reports that were the first of their kind in India. The first of these was a study of child sexual abuse, based on cases in the police records in Mumbai city. Apart from facilitating access to data for the study, police officers also helped us with the analysis. Studying this issue with the aid of the police demonstrated their incisive skills in investigation, and gave us insights into the uses of the law and procedures, which we could employ in our own work. The report by Trupti Panchal and Nahida Shaikh, which emerged in 1997 from the research on child sexual abuse, was a milestone, contributing to understanding its many dimensions and the motives of its perpetrators.

The second project looked into the application of Section 498A of the IPC, which makes it illegal for a husband or his relatives to subject a woman to cruelty by demanding a dowry. This examined such cases in Mumbai city, and it fed into the ongoing debate in the women's movement and organisations on the nature of the law, and its efficacy in resolving problems that women faced. Some papers and studies had questioned the validity of having a criminal law like Section 498A of the IPC to deal with family violence. But women activists, who were campaigning for the Protection of Women from Domestic Violence Bill alongside the National Commission for Women, strongly criticised the police and the criminal justice system for the manner in which it was implemented. On their part, the police felt that women tended to misuse Section 498A of the IPC, often changing their minds after time and energy had been spent on investigations. They also saw family violence as difficult to investigate since it occurred in the private sphere, and thought that Section 498A criminalised family relations.

The Special Cell had in 1998 accepted an invitation from the International Centre for Research on Women (ICRW), a Washington-based NGO, to conduct research on violence against women, and the study on Section 498A of the IPC came under this. We had very rarely resorted to the use of Section 498A, but had intervened in cases registered under it by the police, and recognised the hurdles in the way of effectively implementing it. The research project embarked on finding out from police records what women had said and what the police had heard, and identifying all the bottlenecks in getting restorative justice when Section 498A was used. The report was published as part of a three-study volume entitled 'Journey from Violence to Crime', which came out in 2000.

The third research project analysed Special Cell data over two periods, 1984–90 and 1990–97. The two studies that resulted gave us a profile of the women who had approached the Special Cell, the nature of the violence they had encountered, the other problems they had faced, the kind of help that had been accessed, and the interventions that had been made. They added to our understanding of women's difficulties, while revealing the connections between the problems and indicators of our efficiency. It showed us gaps in the recorded information, gave us an idea of the importance and limitations of the existing data, and indicated the kind of data that had to be maintained. This data analysis helped in further improving our interventions.

Special Cell workers were able to relate to the larger picture that emerged from the data, confirm if the trends and patterns they had observed were right, and recognise their role in what had to be done. It was a win-win situation for all—we learnt from the data and were able to add substance to our arguments for better arrangements to handle violence against women, and we were ready to share the findings of both reports with all stakeholders. The first report, 'Because the Personal is Political', was published in 1997, and the second was included in 'Journey from Violence to Crime'.

The third study in 'Journey from Violence to Crime' was an examination of the non-cognisable offences registered by abused women in the city of Mumbai. The three studies together contributed to the definition of domestic violence that was used in the Protection of Women from Domestic Violence Bill. In 2002, it also led to the creation of a 'drill' for the police to follow in cases that involved Section 498A of the IPC. A significant aspect of the third study was that we engaged in continuous discussions with the police to give our analysis a sharper focus. The police participated in disseminating the report's findings, and incorporated it into the guidelines for investigating cases of domestic violence. In addition, the Special Cell was active in the campaign for the Protection of Women from Domestic Violence Act, 2005, and made three vital contributions to it. We demonstrated what a coordinated, multi-agency response to domestic violence was; our research on violence against women covered domestic violence and had insights from women on the use of Section 498A of the IPC; and we drew lessons from studying the different kinds of responses to violence against women, and domestic violence in India and the United States.

The idea of a Centre for Research on Violence against Women (CRVAW) grew from our experience of conducting the studies on Section 498A of the IPC and on Special Cell data. It became a reality when funds from the Ford Foundation became available to TISS in 2000. Research was the mandate of TISS and its field action projects, and an aim of the CRVAW was to channel research findings on violence against women to multiple levels. The centre supported four research projects across the country. They were studies on family counselling centres and short-stay homes in Maharashtra; on the practice of *nata* among some castes in Rajasthan, which in theory allows a widow or divorcee to live with a man of her choice without a marriage, but is widely misused; on family violence against lesbians; and on the concerns of community organisers addressing violence against women in Assam.

The CRVAW also enabled the Special Cell to accomplish three much-needed tasks. The first of these was documenting the expansion of the Special Cell model to other places in Mumbai city, and to other districts in Maharashtra. The second was undertaking a strategic management exercise in 2001 to aid the process of expansion, and this resulted in formulating a vision statement and compiling a set of monitoring indicators. The third was an independent consultant carrying out an evaluation in 2004 of the Special Cell's strategy and its mechanisms for intervention. The results of this encouraged the state government to consider the Special Cell a 'regular administrative measure' to deal with violence against women, and helped to institutionalise it. At the time, this was one of the few evaluation studies in the world on the subject of intervention in cases of violence against women, as the UNIFEM stated in a workshop on evaluations on interventions on violence against women, where we made a presentation. These three tasks generated a new dynamism in the Special Cell team.

Returning to the Special Cell's interactions with the police, one recalls that they sought our help in cases that required counselling women and men on sexual matters, home visits, and keeping track of women and children who were rebuilding their lives after being freed from violence. They recognised that we had communication skills, were well-informed on social issues, and knew about organisations, schemes and programmes that could provide timely help. The police asked for our assistance when data on violence against women and the work done to help them had to be presented in forums where the force had to be seen as gender-aware. The Special Cell was frequently presented as an innovative service the police offered, and presented as such when they had to put their best foot forward. Meanwhile, in 2004, the Sardar Vallabhbhai Patel National Police Academy included the Special Cell as an agency with 'best practice' in its commemoration volume.

When the Bombay Police celebrated its 125th anniversary in 1989, the Special Cell, aided by TISS, was commissioned to produce a directory of social services in the city for the police. Titled 'We Care', this was published in 1990, and a similar directory for the state was produced in 2010. The unit for audio-visuals at TISS made two films on violence against women. The first, *Sudha Police Thane Gaye Thee* (*Sudha Went to the Police Station*), to be used by the Special Cell in its work with abused women, featured them and the police. The second film, *Breaking Barriers*, was an introduction to the Special Cell approach to work on violence against women. The police obtained the necessary permission and allowed the filmmakers to capture their activities on celluloid.

The Special Cell team was invited to participate in a research project initiated by a consultant to study the police organisation, its administration, and community-building efforts. This indicated a certain level of trust in us. Besides being appreciated for our people skills and ability to analyse social situations, we were seen as non-threatening. Not to mention that the consultant firm got a fair amount of work done by us without having to pay for it.

The Special Cell's interventions in violence against women and its seemingly benign assignments often concealed power contestations of various kinds. But looking back, one realises that the discussions, debates and conflicts with the police and with women's organisations resulted in steady learning, making us conscious of the value of plurality in thought and action. A fallout of this was not taking a crime-centred approach to family and domestic violence. In countries such as Canada and the United States, where mandatory arrests are the norm, the results have largely been counterproductive. Although mandatory arrests protect some women, many are further victimised and seen as perpetrators when they attempt to protect themselves. All but two states in the US have provisions for mandatory arrest (Stark 2007). The US invests an amazing amount of resources in programmes to combat violence against women, but studies show a decline in the effectiveness of the police and the law in preventing domestic violence.

In India, the police do not want to be fully involved in enforcing social laws, and women's organisations—and many women—do not fully trust the police. This led to the Protection of Women from Domestic Violence Act, 2005, which has a coordinated multi-agency response as a key component. It seems as though the real needs of women are finally being used as guidelines, resisting the temptation to lean heavily on the law and the courts.

4

Leveraging the Academic Institution: Role of TISS

Funding, TISS and Other Sources

The policy of initiating interventions in the field was one of the key features of social work education at TISS. This guiding principle was also woven into the curriculum of social work practice. The department of family and child welfare, under Professor M. Desai, started a welfare agencies fund (WAF) in 1956 to raise the funds to support field-based initiatives by TISS and its agencies. The objectives of this fund were:

- Introducing trained professional social workers to work in the field.
- Identifying new areas for trained social work intervention.
- Financially supporting trained social workers in agencies in the field.
- Giving tapering grants for four years to agencies employing trained social workers.
- Providing fees and scholarships to people from the field to train themselves at TISS.

The students and faculty of the department organised film, music, dance, and theatre programmes to raise funds for the WAF. This was a co-curricular activity, with the second-year students taking on the primary responsibility and the first-year students acting as a line of support. As part of the curriculum, students had to learn how to raise funds, organise programmes, work in teams, and interact with the government and the police for sanctions. Their communicative skills were to be utilised to explain their cause to different sets of potential donors. They also had to acquire the basics of budgeting and accounting. The WAF programme was anchored and guided by a faculty member, but the show was run by the students. The WAF had an advisory committee, in which every second-year student was a member. This completed their experience of planning, organising, and contributing to the decision-making on disbursing funds, bringing them full circle. The project accomplished two objectives simultaneously—fulfilling curricular objectives and furthering learning, and raising money for the WAF.

The WAF was the first source of funds for the Special Cell, but the Sir Dorabji Tata Trust, a dependable supporter of TISS projects, soon stepped in. That the Special Cell had been permitted by the police to work with them was considered a breakthrough in stopping violence against women, and raising resources in the first few years was not very difficult. In general, donors are always on the lookout for innovative approaches to old social problems; such sources, though, tend to dry up once the novelty wears off. However, between 1985 and 2005, the Special Cell received assistance from the Sir Ratan Tata Trust, JRD Tata Trust, Bombay Community Public Trust, Hiranandani Trust, and the Raheja Trust. It was also supported by the Gender Equity Fund of Indo-Canadian Cooperation, the United Nations Population Fund (UNFPA), and the University Grants Commission during this period.

Professor Apte's conviction—that social workers in the police system would benefit women who had suffered violence at home—stemmed from her experience of working on a marriage counselling project in the city civil court at the behest of the Bombay High Court. Her vast experience in social work, teaching and research made her a very persistent person when dealing with social and state institutions for social justice. In the very first year of the Special Cell, she opened discussions with the CP to get grants from the state government for its work. Professor Apte knew about the resources within the system, and the importance of harnessing them for social services. For the Special Cell, she obtained infrastructural and administrative support from the police. She was able to persuade the CP to send a proposal to the home department, but this was turned down, citing 'zero budgeting' for the year. This set the tone for answers to requests for financial help from the state government for the next 20 years.

At TISS, Professor Apte and her team continued to divide their time between teaching and research, and writing for grants and funds. Until 2005, when the state government recognised the Special Cell as an official agency and began funding it on a regular basis, it developed on funds from Indian donors. Indian money was pursued because of the belief that adequate funds were available in India, and that they needed to be redistributed in society. It was also a strategic decision because the Special Cell was located in the police system, and the home department was bound to frown on any bilateral or foreign aid. We sensed that seeking foreign funds could leave us open to the threat of being closed down.

Therefore, funds were raised from trusts and societies, while we availed ourselves of central government grants from the Department of Women and Child Development for specific activities like training programmes. In the first 10 years, resources had to be raised every two to three years, and there was no clear long-term strategy apart from wanting the state government to give us grants. Every two years or so, the search for money became my main responsibility, something I did not enjoy all that much. In the late 1990s, the release of two research studies, 'Because the Personal is Political' (Special Cell 1997) and 'Shades of Courage' (Special Cell 1999), reiterated the benefits of the Special Cell's work, including the police's understanding of violence against women. By then, it was apparent that we needed to plan and prepare for an enduring structure, which would be autonomous and support the ideology to render effective socio-legal services to abused women.

To this end, we followed all leads, and networking became an unstated purpose of the Special Cell. The effects of our work were visible, but we needed a vehicle to reach our destination—that of having a long-term arrangement in place. We continued to meet senior police officers and government officials, even as our training programmes highlighted the issue of violence against women. Amid this, the CP sent a proposal for Special Cell funding in 1995 to the DGP, and the additional DGP, O. P. Bali, recommended it to the Department of Home. In keeping with the state government's style of functioning, there was no refusal, just silence. The next year, CP R. H. Mendonca asked if the police budget could be used for the Special Cell, but nothing came of this either. In a meeting with the deputy chief minister, Mr Gopinath Munde, he suggested that police welfare funds could be used for the Special Cell, which we had to politely decline.

All through, obtaining money for the Special Cell from state resources proved difficult. But funds appeared to be available with bilateral and international funding organisations. Meanwhile, the Special Cell team continued to be invited by state, national and international agencies to share its experiences and strategy, which affirmed the need to persevere. So we began exploring the possibility of getting the state government to approach bilateral agencies for funds. But most of the officials were either sceptical or apprehensive of the idea. Nobody wanted to be perceived as 'taking too much interest', which could be construed as their being partial or pocketing a cut. Many women officials, who were already fighting gender battles, did not want to be labelled 'feminists', as that would sideline them.

The Ford Foundation and UNIFEM

Things took a different turn when feminist human rights lawyer Mallika Dutt of the Ford Foundation showed an interest in funding police reforms in 1997. She believed that the Special Cell was a part of police reforms, and was keen to see its expansion. But we had to decline her offer because it came from a private funding organisation. Although the Ford Foundation had funded two large projects of TISS—its unit for women's studies and the rural campus at Tuljapur—its help would have been unacceptable for work with the state, particularly the police. Dutt's conviction and persistence were very tempting. We were looking for resources from the state, which thought of itself as poor, but were turning away money that was being offered on a platter. She once asked me, 'What is your dream, apart from expanding the Special Cell?' My reply was, 'Research, and support to organisations studying and documenting violence against women. Also, to learn from our work, and to draw up strategies to deal with violence against women from that learning.'

In 1998, the Special Cell, as a member of the task force for violence against women, attended its first meeting, chaired by the Additional Chief Secretary (Home), Mr V. Ranganathan. Here, the Special Cell was promoted as an effective strategy by DIG (PAW), Ms Sridevi Goel, and the state department of women and child development (DWCD). This led to spirited discussions, and it was one of the few occasions that the Special Cell team felt it had to go all out to argue its case. At one point, Mr Ranganathan said, 'All this passion and conviction is sucked out once people go into government, and so the Special Cell should not become a government entity.' I argued, 'You and I are also government-funded or salaried, and we work hard and with passion. How can we become doorkeepers and stop the entry of committed people to government programmes?' This came as a climax of sorts, and he turned to Ms Goel and asked her, 'Do you think we should have Special Cells?' She replied, 'Yes.' That was a defining moment for the Special Cell.

At the back of my mind was the possibility of approaching a multilateral agency like the United Nations (UN), from which the government had been accepting developmental aid for decades. But no clear opportunity arose to approach them for discussions. Dutt had struck me as a very resourceful person, and I broached the idea to her, explaining that if the UN or one of its organs like the UN Development Fund for Women (UNIFEM) offered funds, there was the possibility that the government would accept. She responded, 'UNIFEM raises funds from us and other such organisations, they do not have their own money.' However, she agreed to explore UNIFEM's interest in supporting the Special Cell with the help of the Ford Foundation. Knowing about the Special Cell's work, UNIFEM promptly agreed, and this set the wheels in motion. Its regional programme director, her deputy, and the programme officer were enthusiastic about the idea.

UN agencies are by design staffed by local people, and UNIFEM's deputy regional programme director in India was an Indian Administrative Service (IAS) officer, with access to the networks that operated in the government. He initiated a dialogue with the government of Maharashtra. At this time, the Special Cell was ready not only for expansion, but also to be handed over to the government. As a field action project, the demonstration and innovation stage was over, and it was time for replication on a larger scale. This meant that TISS was prepared to withdraw, and it thought that any funds received should go to the police, for them to develop the programme in line with their work on violence against women. Dutt was unsure if this was possible, but agreed to examine the possibilities and met DIG (PAW) Goel for a discussion.

Following this, a meeting between TISS, the Special Cell, Ms Goel, and the Ford Foundation was held at the UNIFEM office to understand the Special Cell's requirements, as well as the police's ideas about this venture. In the end, the police were requested to write an application to UNIFEM for funds. Ms Goel had to seek the approval of the DGP to write a proposal to a multilateral agency. The minutes of the earlier task force meeting, which had been chaired by the ACS (Home), Mr Ranganathan, were instrumental in getting both his and the DGP's permission. Two other factors worked in its favour—Ms Goel had earlier received funds from UNIFEM for a small programme on violence against women, and she had, on her own initiative, attended numerous national-level meetings on the issue.

The Special Cell team held constant discussions with Ms Goel to develop the proposal for UNIFEM. Consultations were carried out at multiple levels and sites, and these were further facilitated by an ongoing training programme jointly organised by the DIG (PAW) and the Special Cell. Talks were held at the training sites with superintendents of police (SPs) and the trainees, drawing on their experience and perceptions, which we felt the proposal had to reflect. Finally, the proposal was sent to UNIFEM, which in turn formulated a plan for funding from the Ford Foundation. The Ford Foundation held discussions with UNIFEM and TISS to ensure that all were on the same page and had a common agreement of purpose.

All of this took nearly two years. While this was going on, in 1998, the Special Cell, after much thought, accepted funds from the ICRW, which came from the United States Agency for International Development (USAID), for research on violence against women. We also heard from the state DWCD that UNIFEM had contacted its secretary to request them to consider expanding the Special Cell model in Maharashtra. The secretary had earlier seen a Special Cell proposal on this when he had been in general administration, and his department had been well aware of our work since late 1993. He later became the state government nominee on the governing board of TISS, and the ACS (Home), after the state government took over the Special Cell programme in 2005.

The flow of information picked up with meetings of the task force on violence against women, and with its participation in a dissemination workshop organised as a part of the ICRW-funded research undertaken on the Special Cell's functioning. These webs of relationships were crucial to our building stronger structures and programmes, and they held firm when attempts were made by different stakeholders, including the police, to dislodge the Special Cell on grounds of procedural correctness. It also led to a better understanding of individuals, which resulted in personal relationships that aided the task at hand.

Since the beginning of 1997, we had been meeting a series of secretaries of the state DWCD at different forums, and keeping these contacts alive. The steady presence and influence of the Deputy Secretary, Mr C. T. Turkar, played an important role in motivating the department to keep track of discussions, department notes, cabinet notes and approvals, and finding appropriate budget heads. His and the DWCD's most admirable achievement came in 2001, when they drafted a memorandum of understanding (MoU) on the roles to be played by the different actors and the flow of funds, and, against all odds, persuaded the home department to sign it.

The Special Cell's advocacy and networking of two years, and 17 years of struggle for funds, culminated in an MoU and validation by the state. Our team's aspirations, conviction and hard work seemed to have paid off, and high on confidence, we were all set to go to the DWCD office on 13 August 2001 when we learnt that the TISS registrar, who usually signed all MoUs, would not be present because of prior engagements. He was obviously unaware of our anticipation and excitement about what we thought was an amazing feat.

Reaching the DWCD office, we found another surprise awaiting us. The ACS (Home) had refused to sign the MoU because it stated that after three years of UNIFEM funding, the government, following a review, would 'take over the cells and integrate them as (a) regular administrative measure'. He did not believe the state had the resources to do this. This dour bureaucrat, sitting in a large room behind a large desk devoid of papers, had refused to acknowledge our presence, including avoiding all eye contact, when we had visited him earlier. His position was forbidding enough, and his refusal to engage in any serious discussion had been another way of demonstrating his power and authority. Instead of him, the Principal Secretary (Home), Mr Satish Tripathi, was to sign the MoU. Since he was very busy, he would just come in and sign, and have no time for ceremony.

Fortunately, the negotiations between the state government and UNIFEM were at an advanced stage, the cabinet had approved the MoU, and the DWCD secretary, Mr Suresh Kumar, a senior bureaucrat, had put his weight behind it. So the ACS (Home)'s opinion did not translate into a decision to back out of the MoU. Something so momentous for the Special Cell team was just one more administrative task for the bureaucrats—yet another MoU or contract to be signed. The only person other than us demonstrating great satisfaction was Ms Goel, who had by then been transferred from her post as DIG (PAW), but was present with a police photographer to mark the occasion.

UNIFEM had signed the papers in Delhi and had delivered them. Those present at the signing were the DWCD Secretary, Mr Kumar; the Deputy Secretary, Mr Turkar; the new DIG (PAW), Mr Prabhat Ranjan; the Principal Secretary (Home), Mr Tripathi; and Ms Trupti Panchal and I, representing TISS and the Special Cell. The TISS registrar did sign the MoU, but later. No details were shared on how Mr Tripathi had been convinced to sign when his senior had declined to do so. All the officials got on with the task, not allowing the setback to derail the process.

Although a lot about what happens in the state bureaucracy becomes known, details of what took place after the ACS (Home) cried off from signing the MoU have not emerged so far. My guess is that the cabinet approval for the MoU proved the decisive factor. This, in turn, had come about because of effective coordination between the DWCD and the police, who were both determined to avoid a deadlock. The IAS–IPS network of personal friendships and similar interests could also have played a role. Plus, I believe that despite not being the DIG (PAW), Ms Goel pursued and contributed to the developments.

When the grant from the Ford Foundation was finalised, it was paid out in two parts—one part, meant for expanding the Special Cells into the districts, was given to UNIFEM, and the other, for the Centre for Research on Violence against Women (CRVAW), to TISS. The centre envisaged promoting a spectrum of activities dealing with violence against women. This included advancing research on violence against women with the support of TISS; funding research in organisations working directly on violence against women; documenting their work; developing more effective strategies for interventions; contributing to the ongoing knowledge building on violence against women; and documenting the expansion of the Special Cells.

Tying up with the UNFPA

Reproductive health was one of the concerns of the UNFPA, and it saw violence against women as a factor affecting this. It was on the lookout for an initiative working on providing relief to battered women that it could support, and invited the Special Cell to work in two municipal corporations close to Mumbai, Ulhasnagar and Kalyan–Dombivali. We had been talking about the idea of 'institutionalising' the Special Cell from around 1998, and had been meeting a variety of people to discuss the issue and find a way forward. The UNFPA was offering us an opportunity to expand our work, along with financial support, and this offer had the scope to make both the issue and our approach to it more visible.

The only worry was that the Special Cell's experience and expertise lay in working with the police system and addressing the socio-legal aspects of violence against women, while the UNFPA's interest was health. Besides, it worked through local bodies and institutions like hospitals. However, the Special Cell team wanted to take up the challenge, and the UNFPA was keen to collaborate with us because it considered us to have one of the best coordinated multi-agency responses to violence against women. This led to a constructive dialogue and negotiations on the locations and strategy. According to the agreement arrived at, the UNFPA would fund Special Cells in police stations within the municipalities. This was our first foray outside Mumbai, and a new opportunity to demonstrate our expertise.

The line of command and the manner in which funds flowed were new to us. The UNFPA funds went to the municipal corporations, and NGOs, which included the Special Cell, had to apply to them to work on women's reproductive health and other health concerns. The municipal corporations saw their relationship with NGOs as akin to their relationship with contractors who provided goods and services. Although this attitude was (to an extent) set aside in the beginning to make room for the Special Cell's services, it resurfaced with the arrival of a new municipal commissioner of Kalyan–Dombivali, who did not see any value in the work on violence against women. He was unable to comprehend the strategy of a coordinated response, and asked how a municipal corporation could fund a service that was outside its control and located in the police station.

In the course of our work, such arguments about who controlled whom created many a disturbance. What was forgotten was that the Special Cell was a service to the community. Looking back, one realises that this partnership, established on the sole premise of the importance of the issue of violence against women, had the potential to develop into a full-fledged strategy in the health system. Unfortunately, this did not happen.

Thinking about this, I realise that one reason could have been the fact that the process of forging relations with the police system outside Mumbai was slow, since this was the first time that the Special Cell was working outside the capital city. It was also new to the demands of satellite cities. The municipal corporations were administrative conduits to the health department, to which we were to be aligned. None of these parties were able to reach out effectively to develop the project as they were all new to this arrangement, as well as to the value of each other's work and the possibilities of what could jointly be achieved. Meanwhile, the UNFPA's policy changed, almost stopping the work. After three years of work, at the end of the project period, the programme had not been fully integrated into the health system, and it was called off. However, UNFPA funding continued to the erstwhile department of medical and psychiatric social work at TISS, which had initiated work at a hospital in Thane district to help abused women with mental health problems.

Expanding to Maharashtra's Districts

Our first experience of working outside Mumbai added to our competence in navigating the difficulties in expanding to the state's districts. Apart from ensuring that the different regions of the state were catered for, the two criteria used to choose seven districts were the rate of crimes against women, and socio-economic features. Funds were available for 10 Special Cells, and the existing three—in the CP's office, and Dadar and Kandivali police stations—had to be supported, leaving resources for seven new ones. The districts chosen in conjunction with the police were Yavatmal, Wardha, Aurangabad, Nanded, Pune, Nashik, and New Bombay.

Our first visit was to Yavatmal. The police there were well aware of violence against women and familiar with dealing with it, but were wary of the idea of social workers, whom they considered 'intruders' or even 'moles', having an office in their premises. They were cordial, yet slow in offering to share their resources. The school of social work was more forthcoming. It saw the Special Cell as a TISS service for Yavatmal, and as a potential employer of its graduates. The faculty allowed us the use of its premises, and was willing to use their professional expertise to help us recruit social workers.

Each district threw up different challenges. The room allocated to the Special Cell in Wardha was near a toilet; New Bombay offered a big, airy room, but had no toilet for women; Nashik could not decide on a place, since the SP's office was under construction; and Aurangabad preferred to have the Special Cell in the CP's office. We insisted that each cell had to be in a place that women from all over the district could access. The Special Cell in Nanded, which had a few NGOs and a school of social work, was the last to begin operating. The police there were highly amenable to the service, but did not have the space to accommodate us. The Special Cell began work under a tree in the compound of the SP's office.

The NGOs in two districts felt that the new service offered by the police was encroaching on their territory. One believed that the Special Cell would draw clients away from it, which could lead to its closure as it had to have a minimum of 100 cases a year if it was to get central funds. The other, which had adopted the Special Cell approach after discussions and training with the Mumbai unit, was also fearful of being on the way out. Their apprehensions had to be allayed, and we pointed out that the Special Cell was only one more service for women who had been subjected to violence, and that it was not a TISS project, but one funded by the state. We tried to reassure them that we were not intending to play the big brother, nor were we keen on driving them out.

Although we had dreamed of expanding, it was an onerous responsibility in practice. Since we had no parallel in our experience, we had to have adequate safeguards in place, identify the kinds of assistance required, and draw on experts to help us identify our strengths and weaknesses. An in-house expert was found, who explained the arduous process we would have to go through to achieve our goals, and the Special Cell team was ready to stretch itself some more. A strategic management exercise group (SMEG) was formed. with one volunteer from each of the Special Cells. While the expansion process was initially envisaged to last six to eight months, the actual time taken was nearly three years.

These processes created a tremendous energy and synergy. First, they gave a huge boost to our aspirations and created amazing buoyancy in the team. Second, the team had to be enlarged, and this meant combing the districts for social workers who were ready to engage with the issue of violence against women, see it through a feminist lens, and work mostly with the police system. This required visiting each of the districts, and building bridges with the local schools of social work, women's organisations, and the police. Putting together a district team took six to 10 weeks. Those selected were put through an in-house training programme at TISS, and had to undergo a module of on-the-job training before they began working in a district.

Alongside this, we held discussions with the IGs in each region to garner logistical support from both the DGP's office and from the district SPs. After a short note of purpose and instructions was sent by the IGs to the SPs, the team visited the latter to explain the purpose of the Special Cell, introduce the new workers, and examine whether the space being allotted for the work was adequate. These activities, and the processes involved in establishing new Special Cells, were meticulously recorded by the documentation officer. While the procedure was more or less the same everywhere, each district presented us with its own challenges, socio-political environment, and individuals who were a part of the 'system'. This exercise was rewarding because it meant articulating the ideology, concepts and strategies of the Special Cell, and drawing on its core strengths to carry out its nuanced and layered work. The process allowed for recognising and acknowledging each individual worker's understanding, which contributed to self-respect and a sense of satisfaction with what they were doing. Many of the Special Cell's strategies were sharpened before they were transferred through training to the new social workers.

While the DIG (PAW), who was facilitating the expansion process, was sympathetic to the issue of violence against women, several discussions and debates were required to explain the ideology and working of the Special Cell to him. He gradually appreciated the strategic alliance, and the approach and skills of the social workers. Yet, he was insistent that he and the SPs, who served as the supervisors of the Special Cells, remain aware of the monitoring indicators that would be used to assess the performance of the units and their workers. He pointed to the pitfalls of not having a standardised assessment tool in the police system to assess the performance of 'non-police' within it. This concern prodded the SMEG into formulating a vision and mission statement, and monitoring indicators for evaluation. The process took a year and a half, but we were all happy with the result, which clearly and concisely elucidated the approach of the Special Cells and their work on violence against women within a feminist and socio-legal framework.

Developing the vision and mission statement and monitoring indicators required ploughing through the years of experience of individual workers with abused women. Both of these were located in a set of values, which were articulated and recreated by each new worker in a new situation with yet another abused woman. Identifying these and separating them from the lived realities of the work was an enlivening and enriching experience for all involved. The exercises worked out by the expert to draw out the fine details of our work were initially daunting, but the concepts derived from the data and experiences were very valuable. What comes to mind is the process of transforming raw sugarcane into sweet jaggery; rather appropriately, the cover of the booklet on monitoring indicators is the colour of fresh sugarcane juice.

While compiling the monitoring indicators, Special Cell workers shared their memories of the cases they had handled, their contexts, and the interventions that had been made. They looked upon their experiences as history, and interpreted and reinterpreted them to come up with concepts that went into creating the indicators. Each worker had to run a fine-toothed comb through her/his experience of interventions and develop tools (with the help of exercises) to separate concepts, principles, values, and specific activities. One of the exercises involved asking workers interested in a category of monitoring indicators to lead the discussion, which was followed by others adding to the subject, illustrating it, and refining the thinking. Individuals had rich experiences, and group discussions enabled an understanding of the many issues involved, imparting new meaning to one's own experiences.

The five-member team that put together the monitoring indicators presented them to 20 social workers, both old and new. A two-day workshop was organised to generate critical responses from them, as well as to provide answers to any questions they had on working with abused women, their families, communities, and the police system. When the workshop concluded, it was clear that the team had a done a very comprehensive job of developing the monitoring indicators. Almost all the issues raised by the other workers could be addressed from within them. In fact, the monitoring indicators helped to train new workers, and added to conceptual clarity among the older ones. The DIG (PAW), who had nudged us into this exercise, also participated in the workshop. In the discussions, each worker stated their own ideological position and that of the Special Cell, both often merging, but each contributing to the evolution of a political understanding of our intervention on violence against women. This lent a sharper definition to the ideology of the Special Cell, in which three strands were visible—social work values and principles; a feminist understanding; and the worldview of workers developed through their individual and collective struggles.

One of the clearest memories of this time was our insistence on using precise language, which would enable a nuanced understanding of our work. Often, a word was chosen after debates and arguments between people whose experiences varied. A dictionary was our constant companion, and meanings, contexts and synonyms were central to our discussions. Each worker wanted to be able to express her/his thoughts and feelings to the women they dealt with. Most of these interactions were in Marathi, and they needed translations and words to convey culture-specific meanings. While we all argued over an apt word, the last mile was usually walked by two or three people, and the dictionary. Meanwhile, the others rested till 'the word' was found. Although these sessions could be long, the participants ensured that the tempo remained upbeat. They were mostly held away from the official space, adding to amity within the team.

All these activities ran parallel to the expansion work. If they had been done before the expansion, we would probably have had a clearer idea of our strategy, requirements and logistics. This might perhaps have meant fewer struggles with the system, and expending less time and emotional energy.

Evaluation Study on the Special Cells

The Special Cell was always under scrutiny from different quarters. To begin with, many perceived it as 'working with the establishment', which implied that it maintained the status quo, did not question inequalities, and worked on the side of power. 'Working with the police' connoted it was coercive, because the police were seen as representing the repressive power of the state. When we began working with the police system to respond to instances of violence against women, it was met with ambivalence. Fortunately for the women's movement, it was TISS and trained social workers, and not someone from their fraternity, who were the 'traitors'.

Yet, since its inception, the Special Cell has been in communication with those it saw as friends in the women's movement and organisations, and it created space for dialogue, critiques and collaborations. Referrals by these organisations, and the increasing number of women approaching the Special Cell, were among the first indicators of its relevance and effectiveness. Relations were gradually built with the police, voluntary organisations, communities, courts, hospitals, and other stakeholders within the city, state, and other parts of the country. In time, the Special Cell was perceived as an innovation worth recognising and emulating. The Central Social Welfare Board began granting funds to NGOs in the 1990s to establish family counselling centres in police stations, and the police initiated similar units in the districts. This was an indicator of the potential of the Special Cell's strategic alliance with the police.

The police allowed the Special Cell to expand in the city of Mumbai, and made efforts to convince the state to fund these activities. They welcomed the involvement of Special Cell workers in many of the welfare activities for their community, which was a sign of their increasing faith in the skills and abilities of social workers to work in a non-partisan manner—something much desired in the police community. We now recognise that even the power exerted by the police to stall the work of the Special Cell reflected, first, that we were getting better at what we did, and second, the force's perception that we were moving beyond its control.

TISS's mandate on research and the documentation on the field action project (which the Special Cell was) further established the role and importance of the services we provided. Both 'Because the Personal is Political' (Special Cell 1997) and 'Journey from Violence to Crime' (Dave and Solanki 2000) affirmed the premise on which the Special Cell's approach was built. The former study, which analysed data between 1984 and 1990, showed that about 6 per cent of women came to the Special Cell after having heard of it over the grapevine, and nearly 16 per cent were referred by the police. The 1990–97 data said that about 41 per cent were referred by former clients and about 13 per cent by the police. Over this 13-year period, a consistency could be seen in a number of indicators and variables. The evaluation study of 2004 corroborated the earlier findings, and provided more evidence on the validity of the approach. This evaluation study became a testimony to our convictions and practice.

The Special Cell team, as well as the abused women who came to us, had faith and trust in its work. There were innumerable gifts of love in the day-to-day interactions with women and their communities—from simple smiles and tears, to sharing and using their limited resources to show appreciation for the support and help received from us. For many, the relationship was one of friendship, built on the shared realities of womanhood. I was once presented with a money plant, sown in a spoon holder, and placed on a saucer. It wrung my heart to witness the gratitude. To me, the gesture also meant that the person did not want to remain only in the position of receiver but had created a space to be a giver as well, showing that we shared the same power. I learnt the self-respect with which women arrived, and was aware that I had to be conscious of their dignity and respect at all times. Warmth and gratitude were conveyed to social workers in loving words and tones, some quite traditional, some not so. All this gave us reason to believe that we needed to continue striving to enable both the women and ourselves to live lives of dignity, with respect for our basic rights in our social and political milieu.

The Special Cells periodically organised 'open house' programmes, inviting women who had used its services to meet over a cup of tea and to catch up on each other's lives. At any given point in time, about 20 per cent of the women responded. Some came alone, but many came with their children, spouses, friends, and parents. Many others called or replied to our postcard invitations, explaining their inability to attend. These were opportunities to receive feedback on our services, listen to women's perceptions about them, and learn of our limitations and strengths. So, they were a sort of evaluation.

In the MoU signed in 2001, there was a requirement that an evaluation be conducted at the end of three years, following which the Special Cells were to become a 'regular administrative measure of the government'. This was an essential condition to get funding for the programme from the government, and for upscaling it to the rest of the state. In 2003, alongside completing work on the vision statement and monitoring indicators, the SMEG team began addressing itself to the need to carry out an evaluation. The Special Cell units were soon alerted, so as to be prepared for an evaluation. Otherwise energetic and forthcoming, the social workers now responded with queries, worries, and even resistance. Suddenly, there was uncertainty, doubt in their abilities, and scepticism over a formal evaluation study capturing the value of intangible gains. Evaluation was perceived as a clinical and distant exercise, and they felt powerless against it. Further, this study had to justify the funds that the state would invest, and it was to be quantitative in nature. Numbers and percentages were to be central to explaining the reach of the programme.

Social workers now began to recollect cases where women had been unhappy with the Special Cell's services, where husbands and in-laws had been dissatisfied, and the questions that had occasionally been raised by the police. They also began voicing their annoyance with some of the women who had sought help, with the system in which they worked, and with their own inadequacies. All of this began to overwhelm them to the point where they began reviewing their work, and being extra careful with their interventions. They also recalled the women who had been unable to get what they wanted from the Special Cell's interventions, the cases where violence had recurred, the women who had been divorced despite wanting reconciliation, and the women who did not want to talk about their painful experiences.

The self-assurance and self-belief that the workers had developed over the years, alongside their skills and capacities, were threatened in the face of the evaluation. Their identities were inextricably tied to their job of aiding women in distress, and the evaluation was to be a test of the value of themselves and their work. For, the exercise would also ask the women who had been to the Special Cell in the last one year what they thought of its services.

The evaluation was nonetheless necessary to ensure the institutionalisation of the service within the state machinery, and we embarked upon preparing tools for it. The creation of the monitoring indicators was fresh in our minds, and these had to now be converted into evaluation indicators. This apparently simple process proved problematic, and the SMEG facilitator had to remind the team about the purpose of the exercise at every stage, while trying to ease their worries simultaneously. This took time and effort, and the SMEG facilitator enabled the team to create a guide to interview women, which was not only incisive, perceptive and sensitive, but also measurable.

While this was going on, the Special Cell was on the lookout for an independent researcher to undertake the task of analysing the data that would be collected. This called for a person with an understanding of the issue of violence against women, as well as social work practice. S/he would also need to be mature enough to deal with the women who had been helped by us, be ready to engage with the police system, and be a constructive critic of the Special Cell. These multiple requirements were not easy to find in one person, and the ones we initially found were either too busy or not interested. Finally, we found a consultant who fulfilled all the criteria and was willing to participate in the exercise. He aided us in finalising discerning research tools, and this went a long way towards alleviating the team's concerns.

The evaluation study was to be based on secondary and primary data. The interview guide was designed to elicit many details, and answering all the questions required about an hour of a woman's time. The research and Special Cell teams had to cope with situations where women had shifted from their previous residences, were out of town for some purpose, were ill or pregnant, were reluctant to participate, or where the husbands and in-laws felt threatened. All these factors complicated the process of arriving at a reliable sample. Social workers had to connect the women to the researchers even as their performance in the day-to-day work of the Special Cell was being evaluated, and the service itself was being assessed. The research methodology and the realities of women's lives made it necessary to lend logistical support to the research and Special Cell teams at the district level.

The study was completed in 18 months. The first set of tables presented by the consultant brought tremendous joy and confidence to the Special Cell team. The report that followed also called for celebration, while providing us with new insights, and a more disaggregated understanding of our work, strengths and skills. It also gave us a better idea of women's needs and aspirations, of what was appreciated, and the small but significant steps that women had taken to rebuild their lives and their sense of being individuals of worth. Each district unit's data showed the profile of the women who had approached it, their needs, what had been done for them, and what else could be done. All of them studied the data for themselves, and reviewed and modified their plans.

The feedback from the women who had sought our help was also reassuring. It also boosted the morale of our social workers, because more than 80 per cent of the women acknowledged that they had received useful services from the Special Cells—57.4 per cent were very satisfied; 31 per cent were somewhat satisfied; and only 9 per cent were dissatisfied. The evaluation study's conclusions were encouraging, and they added to our belief in the path we had adopted, and our determination to continue along it. What we now had to do was present the study, which showed that our detractors were in many ways mistaken, to the government.

The ACS (Home) at the time, Mr A. K. D. Jadhav, was an official who did not believe in flaunting his power just for the sake of it. In all the monitoring committee meetings held till then, he had always been willing to patiently listen to everyone, ask the questions that needed to be asked, and make critical but constructive comments. He recognised the need to respond to violence against women, and had stood by us in our struggles with the other systems we dealt with. The evaluation study report was presented to him at a monitoring committee meeting in 2004, which was attended by representatives of UNIFEM, the DWCD, the police, and TISS. This meeting confirmed that the 'Special Cell shall be a regular administrative measure of the government'.

All previous monitoring committee meetings had been followed by the Special Cell representatives having lunch with their counterparts from the other organisations. These had been occasions to discuss the proceedings threadbare, and voice mutual concerns before calling the office to tell the team how the meeting had gone. This time, too, we did the same, but we were smiling all through lunch. We felt calm, almost light-headed, as though a very heavy burden had been lifted from our shoulders.

The recognition and acknowledgement from the women the Special Cell had supported, as well as from key government officials, made our social workers pay close attention to the women's voices in the study. The key issues grasped were the changes—emotional and situational—that took place in women's lives due to intervention, and the pace at which they took place. This showed the role that the workers had played in them, and pointed to the way forward for the Special Cells. Another point was the need to be aware of the methodological issues involved in research on work with abused women.

However, it was not roses all the way. Special Cell workers had anticipated many difficulties if they returned to the women who had been assisted, and the process of data collection proved that these concerns were not baseless. Many of the women were not happy to recall the past as their memories brought emotional pain and confusion, and some claimed that they could no longer remember what had happened. These responses naturally had an influence on the interviews. Most of the women felt tired or agitated as the questions became progressively complex, or reiterative with multiple responses. The profile of the women and their socio-economic environment often made it difficult for them to understand categories and questions outside their experience or way of thinking. They came across as persons of few words, often not comprehending the need for elaborate and 'unnecessary questions'. From our point of view, questions that involved only choosing between two alternatives, especially on interventions, did not allow for understanding the intricacies and complexities of many courses of action. Methodologically, we were looking for corroboration, but it was not an easy process for the women (Apte 2004).

The women interviewed had approached the Special Cell in the one year before the study. Changes were envisaged to have taken place in their lives at two levels—immediate and long term. The immediate changes were the ones that took place with women expressing their dissatisfaction with the way things were, and seeking the

Special Cell's intervention. The long-term ones were those likely to have occurred over a period of time, following the measures initiated by the Special Cell. These required longitudinal studies if we were to capture meaningful perceptual and emotional changes. And this in turn enabled us to assess where a woman had been when she came to the Special Cell, how long the intervention had taken, the factors that had affected change, and what her present position was.

The evaluation study was a milestone for the Special Cell—after having navigated village and district roads, it brought us to the state highway. It paved the way for the Special Cell to become a state-funded programme, and expand further to the districts. We had believed that our approach had merit, and the study's evidence-based research showed—through different voices and multiple indicators—that this belief was justified. It also opened up many areas for our consideration, and showed us things we could improve on. Despite being a quantitative study that talked in numbers, it spoke a perceptive language. For instance, even though the numbers and percentages were not very large in the section on the emotional changes due to intervention, they represented, in mental terms, giant steps for the women concerned. They reaffirmed that the process initiated by the Special Cell could rebuild women's belief in themselves and their abilities.

The study pointed to gaps in the Special Cell's work, and to the need for increased networking with the police, caste panchayats, and other services. It revealed that the training of social workers had to be upgraded and their office environment improved, while they were encouraged to use their skills meaningfully. It also emphasised the value of documenting case details and building documentary evidence, investing more in developmental counselling, and preparing distressed women for the road ahead through individual and group meetings. A huge gain from this exercise was that each unit was able to identify its strengths and shortcomings. The numbers mirrored the validity of the Special Cell's core work and the sense of satisfaction the women had, which was overwhelming and humbling at the same time. A major lesson was that measuring socio-legal processes and their effects was possible in the given circumstances, and that while such research would give us a direction, it would not provide all the answers.

In 2006, recognising that very few such studies were available on the subject in India and the world, the UN Trust Fund to End Violence against Women invited the Special Cell to present the methodology and findings of the evaluation study in New York to its Expert Consultation on Evaluation Approaches and Methodologies on Ending Violence against Women. The Trust Fund appreciated that an exploration of the evaluation methodologies that had proved adequate to identifying effective responses could help in determining the approaches and interventions to ending violence against women. It also believed in promoting the replication and expansion of effective programmes.

Preparing the Ground for Institutionalisation

In 1996–97, while on leave from TISS, I was at a distance from the work on violence against women, yet connected to the field. This period gave me a chance to work at the secretariat in Hong Kong for the biennial congress of the International Association of Schools of Social Work (IASSW), a conference of social work educators. This was a time when, all over the world, the welfare state was surrendering to the efficiency of money. Changes were on in the UK and Western Europe, while East Europe was opening up to social work education and redefining its concept of welfare. China was to attend the congress for the first time. Political changes had been the fallout of shifts in economic paradigms, which affected the resources available for human welfare and well-being. I got the opportunity to read papers from across the world on the concerns of social work educators, and was introduced to a host of realities. This prompted me to once again review the services developed by the Special Cell, although the issue of violence against women was not very prominent in this congress.

A visit to Bangladesh in 1997 to share the Special Cell's strategy further set me thinking that if the Special Cell had matured enough to be considered an effective organ by bilateral and multilateral agencies, and if the Bangladesh government was interested in hearing about it, then we had to continue our campaign for the state government's recognition and assistance with increased vigour. At every meeting with government officials, the police, and women's activists and organisations, we introduced the idea of drawing on government funds, support, and other resources to battle violence against women. The agendas of most meetings of the Special Cell team from 1998 onwards included discussions or reports on the institutionalisation of its services. When this culminated in an MoU signed by UNIFEM, the government of Maharashtra, and TISS in 2001, we experienced great relief, a significant thought being that we would not have to look for money for the next three years. There was little time to dwell on what would happen after that, because the momentum of setting up new Special Cells in the districts took over.

It did not take long for us to realise that this new phase meant dealing with a new set of provocations, aggravations and frustrations. Till then, we had worked mainly with the police system, with which we had learnt to find ways of handling individual cases of violence against women. We now needed to understand and interact with the state's home ministry and the DWCD to expand the Special Cell programme. At the back of our minds, we knew of the conflicts and tensions that existed between IAS and IPS officers, and between the 'strong' home department and the DWCD. We also knew that the same IAS or IPS officer's powers and resources changed dramatically with a transfer and a new position. But none of this specifically prepared us to conduct ourselves in such situations. Therefore, every time we rowed our boat to various ports of call for the Special Cells, we experienced different currents and undercurrents, if not rough weather.

The MoU required that we have a monitoring committee and a financial sub-committee. These were to be set up by the ACS (Home), who was also to be the chairperson of the monitoring committee. No action of any sort could be undertaken without a government resolution (GR) giving it official sanction. The work on expansion had begun, but we had to wait for the monitoring committee to take decisions on financial transactions, and for GRs. The ACS (Home) at the time was sceptical of the Special Cell programme, and like many others, could not see a role for the home department in work on violence against women. He viewed social services as a soft sector that his department could ill afford to spend time on. He was of the opinion that the issue was the concern of the DWCD and the central social welfare board, and attempted to expand the monitoring committee to include other departments, such as law and judiciary, and social welfare. The invitee members felt that their territories were being encroached on, and believed that violence against women meant marital discord, which had to be solved by counselling, adjustment and compromise—adding to the soft sector myth.

The Special Cell's position was that violence against women, which violated their human and constitutional rights, was a socio-legal concern of the government and society, and that this was well within the purview of the police and home department. Its effort was to establish social services in the criminal justice system, which would serve as a coordinated and multi-agency response to the issue—an aim pursued worldwide by governments, activists, academics, and lawyers.

Thus began the saga of the monitoring committee and its meetings, which were to be scheduled quarterly. On an average, there were two or three meetings a year during the time of UNIFEM funding. After the government of Maharashtra took over the funding and administration in 2005, it came down to one meeting a year. The DIG (PAW) was the secretary of the monitoring committee during the UNIFEM years, but its administrative and procedural work was new to this officer's staff. After the government took over, this role is the Mantralaya's, with the secretary of the DWCD being the secretary of the monitoring committee, which has been renamed the Sukanu Samiti. Every meeting of the monitoring committee held the possibility that we would be introduced to a new chairperson, and to her/his views and opinions, which of course resulted in new alignments among old and new members. It also meant addressing recurring themes and doubts from the members who thought that the police were being burdened with social work, their precious resources wasted on social workers who were intruders in police stations, and that abrasive feminists were breaking up families by talking about the rights of women.

Ripples of this were felt at the district Special Cells in differing degrees. Social workers often faced uncooperative and hostile attitudes when they confronted men about being violent with their partners, and many in positions of power were not very willing to help out. But these workers were resolute in their decision to aid abused women, drawing on the law, the police, and the authority given to them by the state. One simple reason for this was that there was a steady flow of abused women approaching the Special Cells in the districts, right from the day they opened their doors. Their numbers have only progressively increased. At times when a considerate DIG (PAW) or ACS (Home) occupied the chair, we heaved a sigh of relief, and there was a fresh surge of hope and energy. Nevertheless, the whole process was one on which huge amounts of emotional energy were expended. It would not be very wrong to say that the Special Cells experienced their own cycles of battering from time to time!

At the time, Special Cell team meetings were held once in three months. The meetings were for capacity building, monitoring and bonding. But they also served as forums for collective handholding. There were invariably incidents that rocked the boat, and it required a lot of effort to smooth things over. At all times, we reminded ourselves that women in distress were central to us, deriving our patience, courage and spirit from their struggles for lives of dignity and respect. Among the factors motivating social workers were the women who approached the Special Cells, and some policemen at the police station level who empathised with what they were trying to do. There were always two or three police officers in the police stations who endeavoured to understand the Special Cell's objectives and approach, and provided it with support in its work.

The UNIFEM funding was for three years, and this partnership kept many doors open for dialogue with the DWCD, the home department, and the police. In particular, the unflinching support, doggedness and knowledge of government systems of our allies in the DWCD were crucial. In 2004, the monitoring committee headed by Mr Jadhav, the ACS (Home), approved the Special Cells being taken over by the state government, leaving discussion on the structure for later, as the evaluation report recommended. But it obtained an assurance from TISS that it would facilitate a smooth handover of the Special Cells to the government. Despite all this, there was a hiccup, and government funding was delayed for a year. The existing budget from UNIFEM had to be stretched to an additional year, which translated into more trials and tribulation.

Friction with the Police

This discussion on structure proves a major hurdle even today. A new DIG (PAW) and ACS (Home) were appointed in 2005, and both were enamoured with the idea of transferring the Special Cells to NGOs, for different reasons. One reason was to outsource the state's responsibility to groups that were critical of it, using the specious logic of letting a thousand flowers bloom. Another was to make sure that power was thinly distributed, while remaining in a position to distribute largesse. Yet another was to draw on local strengths by roping in NGOs, a process that could then be described as decentralisation.

The new DIG (PAW) possibly felt that the Special Cell's confidence and self-assurance gave his office only limited control over its day-to-day work. The demands of hierarchy and its command and control compulsions being what they are, the police often find themselves unprepared to deal with people and organisations that do not kowtow to their positions. Their unfamiliarity with the vocabulary of consciously non-hierarchical organisations raises the defence mechanism of threat perception, which automatically sends them into attack mode. Looked at in another way, this could also stem from a feeling of inadequacy, or that of being ill-equipped to tackle something they are unfamiliar with.

The post of the DIG (PAW) is perceived as an undemanding one in the police hierarchy—a parking space, so to say. There was a DIG (PAW) in early 2005 who had distantly facilitated a new Special Cell while he was an SP in a district. On being promoted to DIG (PAW), he discovered that the position did not come with a big budget, command over a large force, or power over an extensive geographical area. Working to protect almost 50 per cent of the state's population from violence did not seem big enough a challenge to him. He called us for a discussion, probed us for our thoughts on violence against women, and wanted to know how units to tackle the issue could be created across the state, which would give the DIG (PAW)'s office substantive power and resources. It was around this time that the home minister announced the recruitment of 350 policemen, and there was a suggestion that they be put to work on violence against women. It is not clear if this had anything to do with the DIG (PAW)'s complaints about lack of men and money, but it led to the proposal for what are today called women assistance units in every district.

In mid-2005, the next DIG (PAW) took this forward by giving these units a structure and a mission statement. She visited TISS, held in-depth discussions on violence against women and the Special Cells, and borrowed documents and other relevant material to prepare a roadmap for the units. We later found that large portions had been used from Special Cell documents. Thinking about events, analysing them, and discussing them with various stakeholders, including the police, have led us to believe that granting autonomy to workers is anathema to power-centric persons and organisations. The police leadership often proved incapable of rationally steering through the problems arising from a mismatch of ideologies. And once the power to decide on the Special Cell programme was seen to be in the hands of an IAS officer after the MoU in 2001, all the powers-that-be in the police rose up in protest.

The rumblings and tussle for power strengthened opinion that funds for the programme should be only from one department. TISS had insisted on funds for the Special Cells going through the police, and had envisaged that any procedural problems that arose would be sorted out during the three years the MoU covered. The police saw the DWCD providing funds directly to TISS and other NGOs in late 2005 as a loss of resources. These dynamics of power and control were the most significant factors to vitiate the atmosphere in which the Special Cells operated and interacted with other systems at the time.

Attempts were also made to destabilise the process of the government taking over the Special Cells, with officers writing letters to

SPs in the districts, belittling the work of the Special Cells and asking them to lend only minimal facilities to the units. Another method was questioning and criticising the functioning of Special Cells at meetings with UNIFEM and TISS, and in gatherings of the monitoring committee. This only exhibited the limited perception that most of the police had about the work to end violence against women, and their disrespect for democratic processes. The use of threatening undertones, and their attempts to create doubts about the state government's credibility were considered fair tactics: 'You know how the government functions, do you know if it will really fund this?'

One of the most painful events was the uprooting of the Special Cell from its office space in the CP's office, which had been created to enable easy access to all women in 1984. In 2006, it was asked to move out of the CP's office, and it did so in 2007. It had to shift to the back lanes of the residential quarters for policemen in the CP's office. Many factors colluded in this, although the then CP and JCP were apparently sympathetic to the issue of combating violence against women. TISS's efforts to protect the space of the Special Cell did not produce tangible results because a big battle was said to be brewing between the IPS and IAS cadres. The DCP (HQ)'s office, which had facilitated setting up the Special Cell's office with Mr Ribeiro's approval, could not hold on to it 20 years later because its senior officer did not consider it necessary.

TISS was at the same time developing and delivering training modules and programmes on violence against women to the Mumbai police and the Maharashtra police, while continuing with the work of the Special Cell. In December 2005, the much awaited GR was issued by the DWCD, taking over the Special Cells. Amid our sense of relief and celebration, the reactions the GR evoked from the DIG (PAW) and DGP's offices were not very heartwarming.

Several heated exchanges took place between the DGP's office and the DWCD on funds being routed directly to TISS and the NGOs. We were even called for a meeting by a senior woman police officer to explain 'why the Special Cell had been taken away by the DWCD'. Our explanation—that the Special Cells were now a programme of the state government, jointly in the charge of two departments; that it was supervised by a monitoring committee with the ACS (Home) as its chairperson, the DWCD secretary as its secretary, and the police as its members—did not satisfy her. Stating that the home department did not want to add the Special Cells to its budget did not help either. She insisted that the Special Cells had 'missed the bus' and 'the plot'. This tone and tenor continued to be heard from the police system for another year or two. When convergence was the need of the hour, it was drowned out by the clamour for control.

We met a wide range of officials and stakeholders to analyse and comprehend the situation, as well as draw on their support. We met the DGP, the ACS (Home), Secretary (Home), and reached out to the deputy chief minister, other senior police officers, and friends of the Special Cell among the police and women's organisations. Although our ongoing discussions with the DWCD were a balm to our bruised spirits, our confidence in the police system was severely shaken. We had till then largely experienced the use of police power in connection with the cases the Special Cells worked on; however, this power was now being turned on the Special Cells themselves. It reminded us of the women's movement's refrain—that the police were a force, and caution had to be exercised if things were not to spin out of control. I had heard Mr Ribeiro say during the first few months of the Special Cell that 'measured power on a tight leash' was what we needed if we were not to become a police raj. We were a small piece of the action, but we had been caught in the middle of conflicts and contestations within the police system, and its skirmishes with the state administration.

What helped us to survive to tell the tale are the lessons we learnt—from the ill-treated women we assisted, from our committed team, from the stakeholders who believed in our approach—and the rewarding experiences we had had with the police in the years gone by. The strength to dig in our heels and weather the storm also came from some officials in the DWCD, friends in the police, the women's movement, UNIFEM, and TISS. All of them recognised that we were trying to handle affairs with a degree of maturity, and appreciated our devotion to the cause.

On 12 June 2007, a meeting of the Sukanu Samiti was held under Mr A. P. Sinha, ACS (Home). The police once again raised reservations about sharing space and resources with the Special Cells, and a senior officer (who was not a committee member) was present to lend weight to their arguments. They contended that the DWCD had to augment its budget and create a separate infrastructure for the Special Cells. Both the Special Cell and DWCD representatives pointed out that the Special Cell strategy was supposed to be a coordinated multi-agency response to violence against women, and that being located in police premises and using its facilities were central to the integrity of its approach. After a long debate, Mr Sinha delivered his decision in no uncertain terms. He said that the resources of all the different departments were those of the state government. The Special Cells were a state government programme, jointly managed by the home department, the police and the DWCD. So the Special Cells would continue to be located in police premises, and efforts would have to be made to provide for their requirements. The responsibilities of each department were defined, and the programme demanded working in a consolidated fashion.

Many in the police tended to describe us as 'strong' or 'attempting to be powerful', especially when we had succeeded in raising funds. But that was neither our image of ourselves, nor our reality. On the contrary, we were constantly being pressured by contesting perspectives and groups, who were themselves being pushed around by those above them. The Special Cell workers in the districts were new to the work but sincere in their efforts, and were developing a sense of their own worth. They were often distraught when the SP's office called them and said, 'Empty the room by 4 pm today'; or summoned them to explain an allegation of bribery. Or it was policemen making personal comments, and asking questions that cast doubts on what they were doing. Using psychological warfare to undermine and devalue the work of others was a tactic well known in the police department, but we had not been at the receiving end of this tactic until then.

At times like this, the Special Cell team supported each other by meeting and talking, and continuing to have faith in their work and in themselves. Ms Panchal, the coordinator, led from the front, and older, experienced social workers and our think tank became friends, philosophers and guides for each other.

As the project director, I had my own set of responsibilities in the ongoing institutionalisation process. But I knew that the ball rested in our court—we had the team and we also had friends that we could count on, but it was our grit that would move us, backwards or forwards. Once again, the TISS leadership was proactive and receptive, providing solid backing by believing in me and in the Special Cell team's work. To be assured of support was a necessary condition, but not a sufficient one, since I had to comfort upset workers even as I was trying to uphold the Special Cell's dignity, and my own. I was thinking on my feet, careful to use measured language, and trying to be a responsible, reliable and mature adult at all times. Being honest with one's thoughts, emotions and utterances while remaining critical and detached from the work one was engaged in was the best way to steer the work of the Special Cells forward.

5

Leveraging TISS's Vision of a Just Society

The Tata Institute of Social Science is synonymous with social work education in the history of the discipline in India. The growth and development of the Institute and that of social workers have gone hand in hand for 70 years. The leaps of imagination that the institute has taken in recent decades have been based on its extensive experience of social work education and practice. Looking back from this point in time and reflecting on the role of TISS in the Special Cell's journey reminds me of one of Kabir's *doha*s, which uses the weaving of a *chadariya* (blanket or sheet) as a metaphor for life. Couched in these terms, TISS is the warp and the Special Cell the weft of a sturdy and singular fabric, which has been woven for the use of society in general and distressed women in particular.

Being invited to work with my teachers on a field action project in 1984 was an honour, and there was no question in my mind about accepting it. It was also an opportunity to test whether my capacities were equal to the challenge. Both helping abused women and doing it from within the police system appealed to my sense of fair play. I had worked briefly with a new women's organisation, Swadhar, and the issues on which women sought our aid had given me a sense of the context in which the new project would be situated and developed. Apart from Professor Apte, the head of the department of family and child welfare, and Dr Desai, the director, there were many among the Institute's staff, both old and young, who were encouraging—'You can do it, and we are glad you are doing it' was a sentiment I heard several times. I do not recall having had too many doubts about myself in those days, which is the opposite of what I feel now while trying to narrate the journey of the Special Cells and their work in a relevant and coherent manner.

Support and encouragement from some remarkable individuals and TISS has been a running theme through the past 28 years. I do not recollect a single instance when we went to any of these individuals or the Institute on behalf of the Special Cell and were denied their time, mental or emotional energy, or funds to be used for developing an understanding of the issue of violence against women and intervening in it. From the very beginning, the project director, Professor Apte, and Special Cell workers built on each other's inputs. Although we worked directly with battered women and the police system, our primary location was in the basics imbibed from our education in social work. We entered the system and introduced ourselves as TISS-ians, an identity valued in the context of social welfare and development. We carried our experiences and understanding back to TISS, to be processed with the help of the project director and others, and to formulate plans for future explorations and experiments.

During the roller-coaster ride that the first few months of the Special Cell were, TISS became a place for us to retreat to and recharge our batteries. As in a kaleidoscope, hundreds of pictures come to my mind of the occasions when we arrived at TISS to sort out our thoughts or feelings, or to confer when a situation required further action. For instance, when Project Help was envisaged, it led to a decision to seek the expert opinion of faculty members in the erstwhile department of medical and psychiatric social work. In the Special Cell's day-to-day work, decisions and plans had to be made on the go, and advice or approval often came later, when they were discussed at TISS. Monthly meetings with Professor Apte at TISS or her visits to the Special Cell were occasions to analyse our actions and experiences, and draw concepts and guiding principles from them to help us deal with the next set of problems that abused women or the criminal justice system was going to spring on us. This circle of faith and belief within which we operated not only enhanced our confidence in ourselves, but also heightened our sense of responsibility towards the task at hand.

Professor Apte, who had been our teacher when we were postgraduate students at TISS, performed the role of project director in her own inimitable manner, without ever resorting to imperious ways. She discussed larger socio-political issues with us, which could potentially affect our work, or ourselves as individuals. She had the amazing ability to assess the impact of socio-political factors on individuals, families and communities, and to connect what was seen in the present with what had occurred in the past. For example, when a young Dalit student repeatedly fell ill during fieldwork, Professor Apte recognised that her constitution suffered from the effects of an undernourished childhood. She recommended that the dining hall serve the woman, who had a government scholarship, a glass of milk with a raw egg every day with her breakfast. This was an 'extra', outside the purview of the scholarship.

Professor Apte knew that the staff on field action projects worked against tough odds. They had the responsibility of breaking new ground, innovating, and demonstrating their skills in unfamiliar surroundings, which could sometimes also be adversarial and hostile. Their convictions had to give them the courage they would need in difficult circumstances. Their work was often outside traditional frameworks and required a different ideology, concepts and strategies, and the hours and infrastructural facilities stretched their physical and mental capacities. The salary earned by project staff for new experimental work was not in proportion to the demands made on them. Hence, those in charge of the projects had to create, or allow for the creation of, resources and opportunities for the growth of their staff as persons. Professor Apte demonstrated this by taking a variety of small decisions, which left room for our individual needs and preferences, thus creating a syncretic tradition in the Special Cell.

An example that comes to mind is of one of the early Special Cell workers, who was studying law. Professor Apte made it possible for him to take a three-month study leave, while ensuring that he would return to the Special Cell, which would benefit from his new knowledge. This tradition of providing timely help to social workers continues till today. Professor Apte was able to nurture the Special Cell's work and its staff with a certain detachment; however, nobody felt that she did not care about their difficulties or support them. The initial phase in which the foundations of the Special Cell were laid was intellectually and emotionally challenging, but it was also invigorating, and created special bonds between all who were a part of it. Professor Apte was a valued faculty member, her speciality being her rootedness in social realities, and giving shape to interventions where they were needed. She had the admiration and regard of both her students and the administration. Projects initiated by her were quickly approved, and even her detractors paid her grudging respect.

After earning a postgraduate degree from TISS, I worked as an assistant lecturer at the institute for two years before moving on to the Special Cell project. This period gave me a better understanding of the institute's activities, its faculty members, its ideology and belief system, and the way in which its values were translated into a work ethic. A large part of this coincided with my own inclinations, reinforcing them, and expanding the boundaries of my vision. I forged working relationships with my former teachers, and ventured to discuss and argue ideas with them as a young colleague. Welcoming her students on the first day of each academic session, Professor Apte would say, 'You are my future colleagues', which conveyed the message that everyone could expect to be treated with dignity and respect at the institute. The environment at TISS was thus conducive to critical thinking, and promoted a deep engagement with one's field of study.

It was against this background that the idea of the Special Cell was born. And the evolution and growth of the Special Cell into an effective agency in the battle on violence against women owed a great deal to the support and guidance it continued to receive from TISS. In what follows, I attempt to outline the many facets of our work on violence against women and the ways in which they grew, never ignoring the fact that the institute had a vital role to play in it all. I shall group them under four heads:

1. Developing an intervention programme in tandem with the police system.
2. Training and capacity building.
3. Research.
4. Social work education.

Developing an Intervention Programme with the Police System

Social work training had taught us to respond to the problems of individuals, communities and societies in a holistic manner.

When the Special Cell opened its doors in 1984, we were aware of how to deal with abused women as individuals, but we had to learn a lot more about them as members of their communities, and the ways in which their social circumstances had shaped their destinies. We also aspired to draw on the strengths of the police system and the law, and this too involved a learning process that was steady but gradual.

Over a period of time, we understood the thinking process that lay behind the actions the police took when they encountered cases of violence against women. They often used their authority to force warring spouses to reconcile or patch up their differences so that the marriage would survive, rather than using that authority or the law to stop husbands from subjecting their wives to violence. The institutions of marriage and family tended to be the focus of their attention, even when situations called for women to be protected from violence and crime. Their individual beliefs and socialisation had a greater influence on most of them than what was said in the Constitution and the law, both of which they had sworn to abide by. Paternalistic notions made them forget that women approached them as representatives of the law for protection, and not because they saw them as fathers or brothers. The police's emphasis on marriage, and the family roles and responsibilities of wives, was so strong and unquestioning that our interactions with abused women made us look at the institution of family through a very different and analytic lens.

'Why?' became the question central to our interventions. Why did men beat women? Why did marriages or families sanction it? Why did women tolerate it? Why did the police not file criminal cases against abusive men and their families? Why did the police want reconciliations between abused women and their aggressors? We began looking for answers and explanations, and learning and growing from hearing different voices. Although we initially responded from our stated position, we soon discovered that our varied experiences were subtly shifting and modifying this. Meanwhile, our interactions with abused women, their families and communities, and the police and the law were shaping our ideological position. TISS and the women's movement compelled us to analyse our work with rigour, and helped us develop a feminist understanding of the issue of violence against women. These two factors had a decisive influence on the interventions we staged in later years.

Attending an IAWS conference in Kerala in 1984, experiencing the energy of the women's groups that came together, and listening to the debates and arguments there had opened up new vistas for me. Organising the first national seminar on violence against women in 1987 at TISS for the police, women lawyers and activists gave me yet another chance to learn more. For, this meeting opened the discussions that had taken place between Professor Apte and the two-member Special Cell team, with the occasional participation of other members of the TISS fraternity, to people dealing with the issue from across the country.

The Special Cell programme's ideology, based on a liberal feminist position, expanded to a nuanced understanding of caste, class, region, and religion. We gradually perceived the roles played by sex and violence in the lives of abused women, and this process was aided by socio-political changes and shifting paradigms. All this was possible because we were a small team with a small budget, working on an experimental project that was one of many promoted by a large institute of repute. When the Special Cell completed three years, the police did not call for any meeting, but allowed us to continue our work and grow. Our entry to the police system had been due to TISS, and our continuation was also because of it. The role that the Special Cell team had played involved not rocking the boat, although it gently but surely questioned the hierarchies of power and control over women.

Staffing the Special Cell

From Professor Apte's perspective, good workers were very important and central to any programme. Added to this was Dr Desai's conviction that teams of two were better able to respond to the demands of a project. Her explanation was that two persons could think and act together, supporting each other in the work for a common cause. A lone worker could feel alone or isolated, be sidelined, or become overwhelmed by the multiple demands of innovative programmes. Having experienced this reality, I fully endorse both viewpoints.

To this, I added a few points. Workers had to have the space to develop their professional and personal selves. Both the work and the worker are equally important, and while one may have to be given more importance than the other at different points in time, they had to be seen as not contesting. In a body that aimed to provide a coordinated and multi-agency response to violence against women, team work was an imperative. There had to be a sense of common purpose, the feeling that 'we are in this together'. Even if the roles and responsibilities of individuals varied, it had to be realised that each had its place in the scheme of things.

When I was given the role of project coordinator in 1992, it was initially viewed with suspicion by some, who saw it as having to report to someone who had the authority to push them around. This had to be neutralised by being reasonable, impartial and non-hierarchical, while using humour to put things in perspective. I disliked having to deal with cliques, power plays and backbiting, but it sometimes had to be done. But ever so often the larger vision of being a team with the common goal of helping battered women prevailed, generating great energy for developing new strategies. In short, what had to first be created was a 'we', and then this 'we' had to create an approach. As an educator, I had taught this in classrooms, and needed to practice and experiment with translating it into reality.

We had some norms for the team members, who were contract workers in administrative terms. The workers themselves framed the norms for availing themselves of leave, and for attending seminars, conferences and training programmes, or being resource persons at these. There were guidelines for home visits and collateral visits, which took the abused woman's needs into account. A worker's unplanned absence could overburden her/his partner, which in turn could adversely affect the core work of the Special Cell. The project's fund sponsored capacity building activities for workers in and outside Mumbai once a year, and new workers had to complete a year of work to get this opportunity. We persuaded workers to find a niche area in the work on violence against women, and build their interest and expertise in it. Within the team, we built interest and capacities in counselling, social-legal work, training, and dealing with child sexual abuse, and with children affected by domestic violence. Some workers took an interest in violence against women in minority communities, examining their cultures, traditions and laws relating to these, while others showed an aptitude for research. We also encouraged workers to pursue further studies. All this helped the workers to gain an in-depth understanding of the phenomenon of violence against women. What they had to realise was that the Special Cell was not an end, but a means to respond to violence against women, and that the primary focus was on abused women, not the organisation.

As individuals, Special Cell workers had to imbibe the principles that were to guide their work with distressed women. To work with women, they had to first recognise their own selves, their agency and their autonomy. In the process, they had to examine their positions and lives, and assert the right to live in non-violent friendships and communities. Thus, the Special Cell became a place to challenge norms, and also to endeavour to create an ideal structure to work in through participation in activities and decision-making. Sharing information was a key to building teams that learnt from their day-to-day interactions with abused women and their wide range of concerns.

To me, it was very important to assess who an applicant for work at the Special Cell was as a person, and what her/his approach would be in dealing with ill-treated women. Interviews were a good tool, but the persons who conducted them were equally important. They had to know the existing team and decide if a new entrant would fit in as a colleague and a team member. The other parameters were how well they would adapt to the police system, and their ability to cope with working with abused women and their various problems on a daily basis. There were multiple factors to consider, and the mechanism we put in place was the following:

- Inviting applications, and short-listing them on the criteria of whether applicants were graduates in social work and interested in working with women.
- Calling the short-listed applicants for a group discussion facilitated by two team members, one experienced and the other more recent (to learn the ropes of team building), who followed a set of criteria for observations.

- Another two-member team to interview those who had done well in the group discussion.
- Asking those short-listed from the interviews to spend a day at the Special Cell. This introduced them to the work, its demands, and the atmosphere at the office, and gave them an opportunity to interact with our two-member teams. Thus, the teams could also participate in choosing a new member.
- The project coordinator and project director interviewed the prospective workers after having seen a set of observations and recommendations provided by us. This interview again focused on determining their suitability, with the discussion veering around their beliefs, skills and motivations. The candidates could also ask questions about the work.

The entire process took time, but we were conscientious about choosing people with the right convictions. This began in the late 1980s and acquired definite shape in the early 1990s. In the initial years, TISS students who did their fieldwork at the Special Cell later joined as workers. The advantage here was that they were familiar both with the work and the team, and the team knew them as both students and persons. Knowing a candidate as a person remains an essential criterion even today.

Here, I would like to reiterate why trained social workers are required in the criminal justice system for work on violence against women. Passion, emotion and hard work are not enough to deal with the legal world, and we need persons who are qualified to work in formal systems. The law is a given, and procedures and paths that offer alternatives to women have to be continuously identified. This calls for acquiring some legal literacy and paralegal work. The work is socio-legal in nature, with the women also needing psychological and emotional support to navigate their way through the criminal justice system. In addition, interaction with the police, who stand in a position of authority, requires confidence, and trained personnel have skills and experience to back them up.

The struggle to convince higher-ups of the need for trained personnel continues. In 2011, even an experienced woman activist in Mumbai suggested that the Special Cell employ untrained social workers. This was in part a reflection of the general lack of awareness about the skills and interventions that trained social workers bring in, and in part a reaction to trained personnel asking for high salaries, which most organisations in the social services cannot afford. Yet, the Special Cells have had a large number of their social workers coming from middle and lower middle-class families, and these people have been determined to struggle for victimised women and make a difference, despite their own marginality and vulnerabilities of caste, class and region.

Planning and Monitoring

Planning and monitoring for a field action project seems quite simple if one goes by the dictionary definitions of these words. But what it actually entails can be summed up in the abbreviation POSTCORB + E, which stands for planning, organising, staffing, training, coordinating, reporting the budget, and evaluating. We had no blueprint for the Special Cell project, which was in a way its strength, and to his credit the CP, Mr Ribeiro, did not ask for one, allowing it to evolve (Dave and Dharmadhikari 1987). In 1984, a project proposal was expected, but it did not necessarily have to include the sophisticated data and projections that seem inevitable today. The proposal was in the form of a two-and-a-half page letter written to the CP, which may not stand today's scrutiny, but enabled us to learn and develop over time (see Appendix 1). Each of our initiatives involved the ingredients of POSTCORB + E

Since the Special Cell was a field action project, its every activity was perceived as an occasion for learning—by its workers, the department of family and child welfare, and the police. Such learning included research, and the education and training of social work students and teachers. Thus, planning, monitoring, and the capacity building of stakeholders were integral and essential parts of the project.

Professor Apte visited the Special Cell to attend meetings with the CP every three or four months, and also met the workers. In meetings with the CP, updating him on the work done by the Special Cell took priority, closely followed by requests for administrative support. Professor Apte's conversations were always educative and insightful, and flowed seamlessly from the concerns of individuals and communities to larger policy implications. At these meetings, she introduced ideas on how the police could share its resources, training and experience. This also led to CPs adding their analyses, ideas and solutions, which enriched the project's growth. The loosely structured meetings with the workers included dialogue, debates and arguments. They focused on identifying trends and patterns in women's problems, especially violence against them, and the politics of family and community life. Professor Apte also interacted with our police neighbours, which made many of them better appreciate the value of our work.

In the early days, we (the Special Cell workers) visited Professor Apte at TISS once a week to report on our activities, and discuss our new thoughts, ideas and discoveries. It was also an opportunity to get a pat on the back, and reassurance that we were doing the right thing. This tone of the meetings echoes in today's meetings of workers—every quarter for Maharashtra as a whole, and every month for Mumbai, since this is the place with the largest group of workers. Of course, the items for discussion in these meetings have increased and their scopes have widened, reflecting social change as well as the changing profile and number of workers. These discussions have deepened our understanding of the issue of violence against women, and of the concerns of all stakeholders, including the police. The meetings have also served as important hubs for bonding, team building, and structuring effective strategies to tackle violence against women.

The assemblies of workers signify democracy in practice. New ideas and grievances—individual and systemic—are aired and discussed. One of the ground rules is that all issues have to be voiced at these meetings, where they can be discussed and analysed till a solution is found. There have been rare occasions when this procedure has been used to postpone or avoid decisions; but more often than not, the nature of this process, which brings everything out into the open, results in finding answers to problems.

The other monitoring mechanism was the project coordinator's visits to the Special Cells to observe how case work was being conducted. This often meant becoming a role model, and demonstrating to new and young workers how things could be handled. The focus at these times was on workers' ability to maintain women's agency and autonomy, even as they broke through their mental barriers and social inhibitions. These visits also gave an insight into each Special Cell's relationship with the police, and the way the police perceived the work that was being done. Attention was also paid to whether time was being used with a degree of discipline, if cases were being properly documented, and if the general atmosphere of the Special Cell was congenial, including its cleanliness and comfort. Besides, fieldwork students, who on occasion raised relevant issues, contributed to an inadvertent kind of monitoring.

A peer review was introduced when the Special Cells grew in number. This was expected to promote mentoring and enable sharing strategies to work with women, the police and co-workers. The emphasis on planning increased at this time, and district teams were introduced to it for three to six months. While the exercise began with vigour, the tempo was not maintained in implementation and supervision. The demands of work, while struggling to establish the identity of the Special Cells in different places, did not augur well for precise plans. What we had was a broad outline, and it was our work with women in need that provided it with depth.

Organising the Special Cells into two-member teams, which are reasonably autonomous units, have gone a long way towards giving workers a sense of ownership over their work. The teams took a little time to adjust to each other's ways, but for the most part settled down with or without discreet interventions. Some bonds are now so strong that they are a force to be reckoned with. Supervision and monitoring are not day-to-day matters, and there is very little use of the word reporting. The workers are not cogs in a wheel or one link in a long, vertical chain of command, which would have made them lose their sense of purpose. Their immediate responsibility is to the women who come to them, and they are accountable to the police station where they are based. Their daily involvement in delivering the objectives of the Special Cell defines their confidence, purpose and effectiveness, which also results in making them better individuals.

While the Special Cell teams work hard and even take the time out to enjoy themselves in group leisure activities together, group appraisals have been a challenge after expansion. To begin with, it was perceived as a learning exercise, but with the growth in the number of workers, the ability to absorb feedback from many quarters has diminished. There is now a tendency to see this in terms of attacks by adversaries. In many minds, appraisals are linked to a rise in salary, or power and position in an organisation's structure. Although this was not supposed to be the case in the Special Cell, given its non-hierarchical structure and distinct funding arrangement, convincing individuals and groups about the value of appraisals has become increasingly difficult. Now, being a programme of the state government, there is even ambivalence about how non-hierarchical the structure is, and this goes against one's firmly held beliefs.

TISS would like to continue to engage with the state government, and not give up the responsibility of implementing the Special Cell programme because it believes it has a role to play in making the project achieve a larger scale. Each one of us engages with the state on some issue or the other, and the Special Cell's engagement concerns socio-legal services provided by trained and committed people to aid women who have been subjected to violence. And these services are tools for social justice and empowerment.

Training and Capacity Building

The worker is the Special Cell's primary resource, or the pivot around which everything else revolves. I firmly believe that the three essential pillars that allow workers to give their best are: being committed to an issue or concern; being given the autonomy to work on it; and being provided the opportunities to learn and grow while doing so. In the process, they contribute to streamlining the work and building the organisation. In the case of the Special Cell, this meant evolving effective mechanisms to deal with women who had been physically and mentally harassed by their partners, and strengthening the organisation's sense of mission while expanding its area of activity. TISS helped with the process of capacity building in a major way because it understood the issue, was ready to learn from interactions with workers, and provided supportive supervision.

Programmes for the Police

Training programmes for the police came under our objective of creating awareness among professional groups about atrocities against women. The first training courses conducted at TISS were for sub-inspectors of police and the staff of the Juvenile Aid Police Unit in 1986. These were conducted by faculty from TISS, and women activists were brought in as resource persons. Police trainees at the police training school in Marol, Mumbai, were our second target group. In 1987, we organised the first national seminar on violence against women at TISS for 30 police officers, lawyers and women activists. This five-day seminar was followed by a regional workshop on the subject.

Every time a training programme was envisaged for a level of police, they recommended that their seniors or juniors (as the case may be) be included, implying that while they were doing well, the course would do the 'others' some good. We began to consciously develop our skills in training the police and, with the support of the DGP's office, began training police officers in the districts in 1991. These programmes were jointly funded by the central and state governments. Police academies and training institutes across the country also invited Special Cells workers to train policemen on the issue of violence against women.

The feedback that we received from policemen on our training programmes, which usually lasted between one and five days, ranged from: 'This is the first time I have been back to training after the training I got when I joined the police—and that was 20 years ago', to 'A new subject and ideas that are difficult to swallow. It is hard to change my thinking on the status of women.' Nevertheless, there were many who realised the seriousness of the issue we were tackling, and were pleased to have been considered worthy of learning new things about their work.

Our goal was to introduce concepts, tools of analysis, and data on violence against women. Our aim was not to develop the police's skills of intervention, but to try to add an analytical perspective on gender to the way they saw the issue. We treated them as adult learners, and believed that they would be ready to learn since it affected them and their work. Our faith in people's ability to learn, grow and change was reflected in these trainings, and the response of several policemen proved us right (see Appendix 6). Over the years, we developed training modules for the police, and also conducted programmes to make their trainers aware of the different aspects of violence against women.

Research

Our fifth objective was to document the work of the Special Cells, which was necessary both for its own sake and because it was a field action project initiated by TISS, a deemed university. Towards this end, we diligently maintained the applications that the women had submitted, as well as our registers, files and diaries. To aid in record-keeping and research, care was taken to ensure that a variety of files were always kept up to date. A significant amount of documentation on the work of the Special Cells is in the presentations made over the years to diverse groups, papers presented at workshops and conferences, the publications we brought out, and in the reports of research projects undertaken by individual scholars. In 2003, the various Special Cell units began putting together six-monthly thematic reports. I would like to dwell on how some research projects undertaken by the Special Cell, and on its behalf by TISS, came into being, and how we went about the task of carrying them out.

In 1985, the government of Maharashtra set up Mahila Suraksha Samitis at every SP's office. This was in response to the increasing number of cases of violence against women, especially ones involving demands for more dowry. The local committees, constituted to help with the safety of women, included many prominent citizens, especially lawyers, doctors, women activists, and others involved in social causes. The committees were chaired by the SP and met once in a month. The police presented data on violence against women in the district, and the committee reviewed specific cases to point out lacunae in the investigation, or other shortcomings (Mitra 2000). One such committee was set up in the Bombay

Police Commissioner's office, and the Special Cell was invited to be a member in 1987 by the Addl. CP (Crime), Mr Inamdar.

A monthly report was sent by police stations in the city on the cases of violence against women in their jurisdictions, especially the ones that involved Sections 498A and 304B of the IPC. Cases to do with domestic violence and dowry harassment were sent to the social service branch of the crime branch, and these were collated and presented to the committee. The Special Cell read through every case and discussed their socio-legal aspects with the Addl. CP. In one such meeting, Mr Inamdar suggested that the Special Cell ought to undertake research into the phenomenon of violence against women in the city with the aid of police records. We were eager to do so, and pursued the idea.

Social work students placed at the Special Cell for fieldwork began the arduous task of collecting data and classifying it systematically. At the end of their placement, the job had not been completed, but they promised to work for another six months after graduation to finish it. This set of committed students was ably guided by Professor Murli Desai, a faculty member at TISS, who ardently believed in field and agency-based research studies to develop indigenous and relevant solutions. The next batch of social work students delved further into the data, and interviewed some of the women whose cases had been registered to develop five case studies that helped in the qualitative understanding of the data. Thus, the project resulted in two sets of data—one qualitative and the other quantitative.

Unfortunately, this could not be published immediately because the institute's publications department followed stringent academic standards. The study was placed on the backburner, but in 1997, we decided to take another look at it. The data was augmented with the help of the police, and of activists and friends in the women's movement, and put into a shape that enabled bringing it into the public domain. The book, *Shades of Courage*, was produced by Akshara, a women's resource centre, and released by the CP, Mr Mendonca, at a crime conference of the Bombay Police in 1999. Thus, our first research undertaking was primarily based on police records from 1986–88, and from 1990–95. And they offered some startling figures and insights.

One of the most disturbing facts was that the women, in 40 per cent of the complaints that had been made to the police, were dead. The CP was rather shaken by this, and had second thoughts about releasing the book. He asked us to check the records again and ascertain if the women who were dead had complained to the police in the six months before their deaths. On checking the data again in a police station in the city, it emerged that none of the deceased had approached the police for help in the six months before their cases were registered.

In the early 1990s, Professor Apte thought it would be fitting to have a study on the first seven years of the Special Cell. She envisaged it as a volume that would serve social workers as a reader on violence against women. This study also went through a laborious process of data collection, analysis and report writing. Two factors made this project a protracted one: first, there was just a shoestring budget for the study, which allowed only a few dedicated persons to work on it. Second, it required combining theories on violence against women with quantitative statistics from the Special Cell's records and case studies of the interventions that had been undertaken. We also wanted it to include a small section on the police's role in the Special Cell—all in one research study. This document became 'Because the Personal is Political', and it was released in 1998 at a crime conference of the Bombay Police by Mr Ribeiro, who had retired by then, but remained dear to us as the officer who had opened the doors of the police to TISS to work on violence against women.

A lot of time and emotional energy were spent on producing these documents, both of which, following feminist ideals, had a collective authorship. We wanted them to be seen as the fruits of labour of a collective of workers—to show that the Special Cell could produce knowledge without a hierarchy of thinkers as writers and doers as workers. How far we succeeded in this is arguable, for learning still continues in the context of formal institutions with 'writers' being seen as knowledge producers. All the pre-print work on the studies was done in-house at TISS. A member of the audio-visual unit designed the covers, and members of the unit for women studies helped with the title—'Because the Personal is Political'. The books were printed by the press that did TISS's annual reports.

For the Special Cell team, the publication of these two works was a milestone. We were able to convincingly traverse two worlds—those of fieldwork and research. Almost all the workers at the time of the studies contributed to the research process. This was done in two ways—by continuing the work with the women who came to the Special Cell; and by bearing the burden of the work of those who were away, helping with the research. Such invisible contributions are often not acknowledged, and that was one of the reasons why the names of all Special Cell workers appear in an annexe—an idea taken from 'Our Bodies Ourselves', written by the Boston Health Collective (1992), which I first saw in the mid-1980s.

The energy generated by this high point set the scene for including research as an integral part of the work of the Special Cell. The next two studies were on cases of child sexual abuse reported to the Bombay police, and on arbitration in cases of domestic violence by Jat panchayats, using customary norms. The Special Cell team was enthusiastic and wanted to be trained in qualitative research methodology—both to develop their documentation skills and to participate in research projects. There was a steady stream of requests to look at Special Cell data from faculty colleagues, doctoral scholars, and organisations involved in work on violence against women. In 1997, the ICRW invited the Special Cell to share its data by undertaking a research project. As mentioned earlier, the funding was to be from USAID, and I had doubts about using international monetary support for research while we were based in the police department.

Much pondering and discussion took place with the team and with colleagues at TISS. During this time, a new coordinator took over at the ICRW, and she was keen that we be the principal researchers, coaxing us to embark on the project. Finally, we decided to take the plunge. An important consideration at the time was the opportunity to look at Special Cell data anew. We wanted to explore the possibility of finding answers to many more questions on violence against women that had emerged in our minds. Two other faculty members at TISS were also roped in by the ICRW to participate in the project. The culmination of all this was a research proposal for a two-part study on, first, identifying patterns and trends in domestic violence from the records of the Special Cell, and, second, the nature of the violence that women were subjected to, and its reflection in police records.

This was the first time that I was to formally lead a research team. We requested Gopika Solanki, a colleague in the department of family and child welfare, to join us on the research project. Having been a social work student who had done her fieldwork at the Special Cell, she had experience and knowledge of what we did, as well as an inclination for research and writing. She proved to be the backbone of the research process, and also took the lead in writing certain parts of the report. Over a two-year period, we read and unravelled our files and police records, and sharpened our understanding of the law and its processes. The issue of the police, who are trained to protect citizens from violence, overlooking the basic rights of women in cases of domestic or sexual violence (which left them even more vulnerable), came up once again. On the whole, we attempted to understand what women's concerns were, and the extent to which the services offered by the Special Cell matched their needs.

The findings were encouraging, but the research process revealed that the Special Cell's documentation was not as meticulous as it should have been. There were questions we asked about its practices, only to find that the data had not been recorded in a reliable manner. About 20 per cent of the responses had to go under the category of 'not available'. The immediate effect of this was that the registers were changed, with the entries in them made more detailed. There was also a greater resolve among both workers and supervisors to be more careful about recording all relevant information.

The study of police records also led to an engagement with the crime branch of the Bombay police to develop a 'drill' for the police in cases where Section 498A of the IPC applied. This was an idea of the CP, Mr Mendonca. In 2000, the ICRW conducted a national conference in Bangalore on studies on violence against women, in which representatives from the police, the hospitals, courts, and NGOs participated. This was in part meant to disseminate the findings of our research study. It was important to me that the police participated because they were, in a way, partners in the research, who deserved to be given the dignity and autonomy they were often denied in the police system. And they had to have opportunities for learning more if they were to protect women from violence.

I pursued the CP to convince him to depute seven officers from various levels of the crime branch to attend the conference—a police sub-inspector, three inspectors, the head of a police station, the head of the social service branch, and the Addl. CP (Crime). The CP was reluctant to let seven officers go to Bangalore at the same time for a conference; however, when our request had to be approved on paper, he was away on leave for his daughter's wedding. The joint commissioner of police signed off on all seven officers attending the conference, although he himself had to drop out because he was holding charge of the city of Mumbai. In all, eight studies were presented at the conference, which was a high-profile event on violence against women, attended by people from all walks of life and covered extensively in the media. It enabled us to forge professional alliances with several individuals and institutions. Translating ideas and values that one holds dear into reality is always challenging, but when it does happen, it is exhilarating. With it comes a sense of affirmation that convictions are worth standing up for, even if it means working hard.

The two-part study had findings backed by the police and Special Cell records, and this added to our ability to dispute statements made only on the basis of opinions or biases, or out of sheer stubbornness. But we continued to hear people say things like, 'This data is of Bombay city. Urban, rural is different, madam.' The ICRW had commissioned two sets of studies in India, one on best practices and the other on an analysis of records. Our study fell under the second set. The centre had also put a few measures in place to guide and monitor the research teams. There was a national advisory body of well-known academics, activists, and practitioners such as lawyers, doctors and police officers. Every three or four months, the researchers met the panel at different places to brief it about their work and to receive critical feedback. This also led to constructive interactions with members of the group. In addition, the meetings brought all the research teams together on a common ground for mutual learning, and many new relationships were built at these times.

The ICRW's project of violence against women in India was part of a larger project funded by USAID for research activities in many other parts of the world. We therefore had the opportunity to meet and listen to scholars from many parts of the world, once in India and the second time at a conference in Washington, DC, in 2000 to mark the end of the large project. Our study, entitled 'Journey from Violence to Crime: A Study of Domestic Violence in the City of Mumbai', was produced by the department of family and child welfare at TISS in 2001. This study, and two others from TISS—'Domestic Violence as a Public Issue: A Review of Responses' by Nishi Mitra, and 'Examining Health Records for Evidence of Domestic Violence: A Research Study in Maharashtra, India' by Surinder K. P. Jaswal—have become a part of the larger discourse in the country on violence against women. We were invited by many organisations to present our findings, and the study was translated into Hindi by Purva Yagnik in 2004 for a women's resource centre in Rajasthan.

It was from this research project and the dissemination of its findings that the idea of the CRVAW was born. The close linkages between the Special Cell's activities (services and research), its location (TISS and the police system), and the need for socio-legal work to assist abused women continued to create synergy.

Centre for Research on Violence against Women (CRVAW)

Hungarian biochemist Albert Szent-Gyorgyi once said that research was seeing what everybody else had seen, and thinking what nobody else had thought about it. The genesis of the CRVAW in 2000 can be traced to such a notion. Long years of engagement in the field with the issue of violence against women meant that a lot had been witnessed, but that it was now time to think differently and critically about it. It was time to widen our horizons.

It is important to understand the CRVAW against the backdrop of the long years of work undertaken by the Special Cell. The centre evolved out of the research and documentation carried out by the

Special Cell, and from the realisation in the course of its work of the need to look at all the relevant socio-legal aspects of policing violence against women. It was hoped that the data that had emerged in earlier studies would help to throw light on a range of issues, which could feed into the possibilities for further research and interventions.

Both the state and the voluntary sector in India require systematic data collection on social issues and their analysis, which can then be put to good use by the systems that exist. Often, large amounts of data get lost in the bureaucratic labyrinths of the state machinery. Studies undertaken on specific issues meet the same fate, because their findings are unacceptable to different stakeholders in the criminal justice system. There is a reluctance to accept scientific enquiry, be it in the form of research findings, studies, statistics, or documentation. The inclination is to look at research findings in parts, localising a problem and ignoring its wider ramifications. The Special Cell's engagement with the Bombay police had given it a vantage point from which to observe and understand the police system, and its attitudes and practices. Hence, it was in an advantageous position when it came to thinking about attempts at systemic changes.

At the Special Cell, individual and collective work experiences had many a time been documented in the form of small studies and papers. The data had essentially been from the PC's office. Over time, we realised that we had to expand the scope of research to explore other relevant socio-legal dimensions of the issue that we dealt with on a daily basis. There was a need to not only gather the data that was available, but also develop research skills to interpret facts and figures in a more meaningful manner.

The CRVAW began work in December 2000. In the five years of its existence, it explored new fields of research, as well as new frontiers of methodologies in research. Responding to dynamic realities in the field and ensuring a multi-disciplinary approach to studying them involved setting up the infrastructure and administrative system suited to this, as well as forming a team of dedicated social workers. The emphasis was always on the mutual and collective learning that occurs as we proceed to understand complex realities.

Years of activism and mass movements have ensured that gender is now a factor considered in matters of policy, planning and intervention. There is now an attempt to mainstream women's concerns, which are not immediately dismissed, as they used to be before. However, in these years, we have also seen how the establishment has become more creative in subverting pertinent issues. At a recent training programme for senior police officers in the country, violence against women in the family continued to be perceived in terms of 'there can never be equality of genders in India', completely disregarding the oath the police had taken to protect all citizens from violence. The officers not only communicated their ideas about the position of women in our society, but also endorsed their unequal citizenship. While these perceptions are not new, what has to be noted is the unrelenting nature of these attitudes and opinions, born out of popularly held sexist ideas and unexamined biases.

We were in agreement that nothing far-reaching could be achieved without forming alliances with other NGOs. Towards this end, we remained in touch with different organisations and individuals to engage in an exchange of findings and material on violence against women. Further, small and independent research projects were undertaken, according to the needs of the subject and the institution. It was crucial to effectively disseminate the findings of the studies undertaken, and make their reports available to the groups interested in them. Such dissemination, we believed, was essential to ensure that research findings were integrated into the functioning of NGOs, the judiciary, the police, academic institutions, and policymakers. Some of the studies were also translated from English to Marathi to enable them to find a larger audience.

The studies undertaken by the centre covered myriad groups of women with different needs; all of them, however, were linked through their common experience of violence. There were studies on violence faced by lesbian women, and women in Rajasthan, and the custom of *nata*, among others. This served to not only understand the different dimensions of violence, but also confirmed the surmise about the pervasiveness of violence in women's lives. The centre also produced documents for dissemination and training purposes. Training programmes for the police on gender issues, violence and the law, which began in 1986, continued to be an important component of both the Special Cell and the centre's work. Various voluntary and state organisations showed an interest in understanding our experiences with conducting training courses for members of the Maharashtra police.

One of the obstacles the centre faced was the lack of interest often shown by stakeholders whom it considered important to a project. It was important to conceptualise more participatory processes that invited diverse perspectives, but many of these seldom translated into actual participation. On a more reflective note, the centre's projects could have drawn on people, NGOs, or voluntary organisations whose work did not deal directly with gender issues, although it concerned them. However, from what we saw, help was not very forthcoming from this section, either. Research on the socio-legal aspects of cases on violence against women that went to court could also not be initiated because of a lack of people with the necessary inclination.

Around the third year of the project, a need was felt to extend it for some more time. The extended project period was necessary to organise the reports and disseminate the copies to the stakeholders. Given below is a list of studies and documents brought out by the centre.

1. Bina Fernandes and Gomathy B., *A Study on Violence Faced by Lesbian Women*, 2003.
2. CRVAW, *A Study of the Special Cell for Women and Children, 1997–2001*, 2003.
3. Neela Dabir, *Violence against Women: A Study of Family Counselling Centres and Short Stay Homes*, 2003.
4. Meena Deval, *A Handbook for Abused Woman* (*Me Mazhich*, in Marathi), 2003.
5. CRVAW, *Profiles and Perceptions of Workers at the Special Cells: An Inquiry into the Understanding of Feminist Social Work Intervention*, 2004.
6. Meghali Senapati, *Position of Women's Issues and Violence against Women, in the Practice of Community Organisation, in Assam: A Process Document*, 2005.
7. MJAS, *Violence against Women, as a Result of Customary Remarriage Practice of Nata, in Rajasthan*, 2006.

The research work undertaken by the centre was painted on a larger canvas than merely that of domestic violence. This led to a more nuanced understanding of the pervasiveness of violence in women's lives and the nature of gendered violence. The first three years of research and documentation recognised and affirmed the need for focused attention on building an indigenous knowledge base on violence against women on the part of practitioners as well. The centre's work, especially its support in terms of research, training and intervention in violence against women, were recognised more widely, and requests for support started coming in from various external agencies. The only glitch was that all of this took place around the fourth year, when the project was in the process of winding down its activities.

This clearly pointed to the need for setting up a resource centre for research, training, policy support, and intervention in violence against women for the police system. A sustained and critical engagement gave the centre a sense of the problems that had to be fixed, to ensure that the violated women who approached the police or the courts actually obtained justice. It believed that it was important to have a nodal agency that could house a resource centre for the police and the courts, which the women could easily access for their needs. There was the hope that at the end of the project period, a clearer direction would evolve, which would consolidate its achievements and at the same time be responsive to future developments.

It has to be mentioned that it is never easy to conduct research in the area of violence against women. Research often has to take a back seat when the priority is responding to the immediate needs of women in distress. Also, studying the issue of violence is perceived as a threat to family unity, and to community and cultural identity, so much so that many communities keep scholars away from their women. Women are also reticent about speaking out in the face of hostile reactions from their families and communities. Some women's organisations—and abused women themselves—are not always willing to brave the issue of violence because they see other concerns, such as family and social relations, as more important.

At the organisational level, documentation and research are not considered essential in an organisation's development, even when they could fulfil important needs and purposes. There is also a dearth of researchers to work on the subject of violence against women. A considerable amount of time is expended on the execution, coordination and administration of projects, leaving little time for innovation and creativity in research. After a candid appraisal, we feel that there are still whole sets of ideas and issues that remained unexplored.

Any retrospective would be inadequate if it did not look at the low points, at the moments that taught us something valuable. In the course of our journey, we realised that we perhaps needed to be a bit more realistic about research not being a priority for all the staff in a field-oriented project, especially because they already had demanding schedules. We also learnt that it is difficult to find trained and competent people with an inclination for research. And last, but not least, we had to recognise that preparing people and contexts to embark on the complex task of being 'interventionist researchers' was a Herculean task.

The interesting thing about our journey was that every time we brought closure to a project, it opened up a new opportunity to understand yet another aspect of violence. Between 2000 and 2005, our research and expansion activities went hand in hand, creating a ripple effect. In 2006, the project Access to Justice, under the aegis of the United Nations Development Programme (UNDP) and the central government, invited us to demonstrate the Special Cell approach in Haryana and Madhya Pradesh, extending its reach to the north. This experience, along with organising and implementing the Special Cells in Maharashtra, led us to think of ways to lend a unity to the work that was branching out in many directions, and we decided that the way forward was setting up the Resource Centre for Intervention on Violence Against Women. This was done in 2008, and it was housed in the school of social work at TISS.

Social Work Education

From 2004 onwards, TISS began the process of reconstructing itself to become even more relevant as an institution of higher education in a society that was changing rapidly. It wanted its social work education curriculum to reflect this by bringing in new ideas, methodologies and structures to address social issues. Debates and deliberations among faculty members culminated in the identification of three new fields of practice for social work—Dalit and Tribal Social Work, Disability Studies and Action, and Women-Centred Social Work.

Before coming to my involvement in this process, it would be pertinent to say that 20 years of deep engagement with the issue of violence against women had led to a greater insight into the sources of women's oppression. This was the impetus behind contributing to building a curriculum that would produce critical and effective social workers to address the issue of women's subordination. The institute's field action projects were developed to teach and practise social work. They were to provide a space in the university system for experimentation and innovation—a social work laboratory of sorts for teachers and students, to practise in and learn. They were also an affirmation of the belief in planned change, in social work principles and values, and a training ground for facing the many dilemmas that were bound to come up, and resolving them. A large number of students have taken their first few steps in social work in a field action project. My first fieldwork placement as an undergraduate was in one—the Municipal School at Danda, a field action project of the College of Social Work, Nirmala Niketan, in Mumbai.

The Special Cell's contribution to social work education is what I would like to begin with, and then work backwards to what social work education contributed to the individuals who drew on it to develop the programme for violence against women. One of the distinct things that the Special Cell did was recognise women as a category for analysis, learning from the changing environment created by women's movements, and observing 1975 as the international year of the women. When I studied social work between 1977 and 1982, what was addressed was women's 'condition', not their position. The only course taught separately at TISS on women was 'Women's Welfare', which dealt with government schemes and programmes to help women. When I attended the first three national conferences of the IAWS, I found that it had little to do with what had been introduced to me in the curriculum. It was more in the spirit of participating in a movement of my interest, and this had been imbibed from social work education.

In the section on setting up systems for the Special Cell, I detailed the influence of social work training on our actions. Here, I would like to recall an invaluable lesson learnt from social work—to use your knowledge for people-centred development, you have to continue to strive to bridge the gap between individual values and principles, and those of social work. That the personal is political is something I learnt from working on violence against women.

Consequently, social work education, both in the classroom and the field, opened up new realities to students. Those who came to the Special Cell for fieldwork from the department of family and child welfare at TISS developed a critical lens through which to look at social work itself. Standing in distressed women's shoes and looking at social work education from the outside made many of them realise that the curriculum had given them an inadequate political understanding of the category of woman. Seen in this light, social work, as taught in the classroom, seemed a benign and ineffective discipline. The reality of working with women, and the individual and group discussions that introduced them to a feminist perspective, came as a revelation.

Workers in the Special Cell and the supervisors of students also gained from student placements. It was an ongoing education for them, for they had to be on their toes to explain standpoints and interventions. They also had to field critical comments on the work from their students, who were young adults full of enthusiasm, idealism, and a belief in their ability to 'change the world'. Special Cell workers received new ideas and perspectives that the students brought in from the classroom, and from their readings and discussions. The students brought the Special Cell to life by their readiness to do even mundane tasks, like arranging reference material and files, and updating the correspondence. They organised an 'open house', got together material for training programmes, shared in all the work, and lifted everybody's spirits with their witticisms. In 1988, a batch of three students initiated a Special Cell in the Thane PC's office; the batch of 1997 began the process of documenting the strategies of the Special Cell; while others reached out to groups affected by violence that we had so far not approached.

In short, students who did their fieldwork at the Special Cell not only learnt what they did not know, but also brought to us their observations, questions, dilemmas, and delights. My growth as a social worker was built around my work with violated women, with the Special Cell as its fulcrum. Social work education gave me an abiding belief and faith in the human spirit, and in its innate capacity to create and survive. At the Special Cell, helping abused women gave this belief a focus. The engagement was both revealing and overwhelming, giving me a clear idea of the social mechanisms that exerted a coercive control over women. This control was exerted not only over their thoughts and emotions, but also over their knowledge and wisdom. I continuously attempted to bring these understandings to the classroom, and to encourage students to think and reflect for themselves. They had to be enabled to interpret their life experiences, analyse them, and act on them, while always appreciating and valuing the characteristics that women were endowed with. However dismissive a patriarchal society is of them, it is women's emotional, physical and sexual work ties that bind families and communities together—through sustenance, production and reproduction.

Being a deemed university, TISS gave its faculty members the autonomy to explore and try out new methodologies for teaching and learning. In 1986, Professor Apte began a seminar course focusing on 'Women's Issues, Policies and Programmes'. Our combined understanding of women's issues, social work education, and the methods and principles to be used in the classroom brought about a metamorphosis in teaching about women as a subject. In other words, we gave the curriculum a gender lens. The method was intended to overlap and repeat what had already been learnt. Students presented their papers one by one each week, and their audience connected to them from their experiences. New thoughts and questions evolved during the readings and discussions in the classroom, as well as outside. In all, it was a collective attempt to answer each other's questions, and it allowed me to remain young in spirit. I had to search for answers along with the students, and try to honestly gain the respect of their bright minds.

In the classroom, a maxim of mine used to be, 'You begin with women, but you do not end with them'. The sentiment behind this had an opportunity to bloom in 2006, when the school of social work put me in charge of the curriculum-building exercise for the field of Women-Centred Social Work (WCSW), converting a two-credit course into a 12-credit programme. Once again, the experience of working with the Special Cell made me dig deep into the realities of women's lives to see how this knowledge could be used to craft the programme, and mould social workers with aspirations, who could make a difference to the world of women. The general outline of the WCSW emerged from the deliberations and debates of a small team of faculty members, and it included a specific course on 'Gendered Body Sexuality and Violence'.

Figure 5.1: Conceptualisation of Women-Centred Social Work and its Objectives

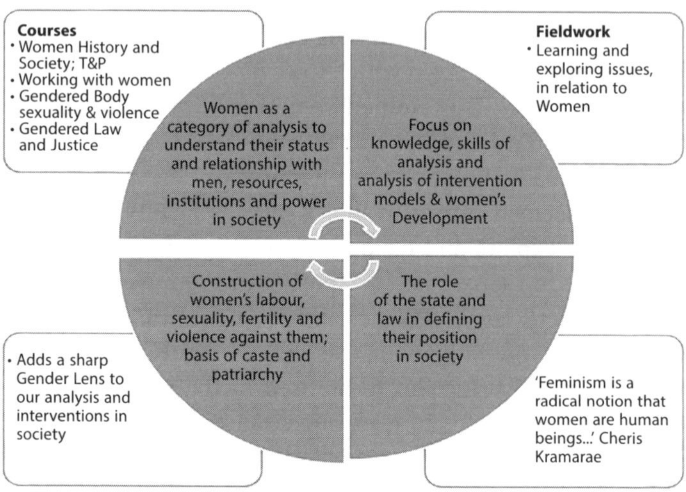

The Special Cell, as a field action project, was introduced in most refresher programmes organised for social work teachers by the social work education cell at the TISS. But many of these teachers did not consider the Special Cell, women, or violence against women as serious subjects of study. Upon reflection, it occurs to me that resources, both tangible and intangible, are limited in the social work community, and that social work as a profession has yet to gain a meaningful status in the country. We are yet to make a mark in providing social work in situations that demand it. In the context of the Special Cell, I can only remember two instances when this happened. Two police officers from Mumbai, who had helped in setting up Special Cells in the state capital, continued the good work when they moved out—one, as CP in Nagpur, initiated talks in 1995 to start a Special Cell there, and the other, as SP in Satara, took the lead in establishing a Special Cell there in the late 1990s.

Due to the training programmes it conducted for them, TISS became a platform from which the Special Cells could interact with senior police officers and bureaucrats across the country. Communicating with both networks that could effect change—the senior police officials (IPS) and senior bureaucrats (IAS)—provided a vital opportunity to explain the necessity of the strategic location of the Special Cells to address the issue of violence against women. An article on the Special Cells was included in a volume on the best practices of the police, published by Sardar Vallabhbhai Patel National Police Academy, Hyderabad. Apart from the police, the value of social work with abused women was introduced to health professionals, social work educators, para-professionals, and administrators in different parts of the country.

Engaged as both a Special Cell worker and a social work educator, I was interested in seeing education acquire a holistic meaning. The work of the Special Cells was an exercise towards this—by working with women and with people in systems, and with social institutions and structures, from where it flowed into classrooms and to students. I have come to realise that social work education has to be political, while facilitating the development of skills of analysis and intervention. It is all about understanding the disaggregated pictures and looking at their finer details to identify avenues for interventions and programmes, without losing sight of the larger holistic picture. And social work training is about pursuing one's passion for social justice in a disciplined manner.

TISS was one of the pillars on which the work on violence against women rested. All its offices, right from the administrative office to the director's office, have played a role in sustaining the Special Cells. Its governing board and chairpersons have shown an interest in facilitating processes by putting in a good word in high places from time to time. All its heads and directors have, to some degree, been engaged with the Special Cells. The institute has essentially stood by the Special Cells, and in a sense, owned them. A new faculty member with years of field experience summed up the relationship when she said, 'It says a lot about TISS that it nurtures field action projects like the Special Cells and Prayas .... It is a university with a political engagement.'

TISS has always been a place for direct and indirect interaction with a wide variety of ideas, people and ideologies. Its alumni often say that learning at TISS meant learning from a wide variety of sources, many of them outside the classroom. Colleagues—faculty members, and administrative and service staff—occasionally used the services of the Special Cells, gaining their respect for its effective presence.

Of course, debates on field action projects versus research continued, creating not only hierarchies, arguments and learning, but also displeasure among the field staff. Getting stuck in either-or arguments, such as 'Field action projects have led to research, but most research has not led to social change', was in the ultimate analysis quite futile. The Special Cells have been able to demonstrate that social workers with the skill to analyse situations and intervene can be effective, and also convince the state of the necessity of employing trained social workers where they are required. But every so often, the finances required to pay trained personnel queer the pitch. Although the government invests in social work education, it unfortunately does not seriously consider harnessing these graduates in programmes for social justice and efficient governance. It tends to count costs in terms of immediate payment, not seeing it as an investment or trying to discover the cost-benefit advantage that is initially not so apparent.

This space, which has been created for me to reflect on the Special Cells and write an account of their journey, is essentially a fallout of my association with TISS. Field action projects are a part and parcel of social work education and practice, and not ends in themselves. One of their essential duties is to be able to continuously ask, 'Why are we doing what, and what did we do why?' (Desai et al. 2000).

6

Back to the Present: The Way Forward

Engagement with Policies, Programmes and Laws

The year 2005 was a milestone for the Special Cell programme. It saw the transformation of what had begun as an experiment in providing essential services to women in distress into a full-fledged programme of the Government of Maharashtra, which provided socio-legal services to women who had been subjected to violence by their partners. This coincided with the enactment of the Protection of Women from Domestic Violence Act, 2005. This Act recognised the need for, and importance of, having a coordinated and multi-agency response to violence against women, while acknowledging the role of women's organisations and other social service institutions as service providers. It also envisaged building bridges between agencies working for the cause of abused women, and widened the definition of domestic violence to include more types of violence and more categories of women.

Importantly, the role of protection officers and service providers was modelled on the work of the Special Cells in Maharashtra, which was one of the few bodies in the public domain extending meaningful support to abused women. Situated in the police system, the Special Cells had a vast experience of working on cognisable and non-cognisable cases of domestic violence. Women had turned to it after complaining to the police, or registering cases in family courts. The Special Cells had also participated in negotiations and arbitration to stop violence against women. We were able to use this knowledge to work alongside the network of women's groups campaigning for the Protection of Women from Domestic Violence Act. The Special Cells organised and participated in a number of meetings, the first of which was conducted by the

National Commission for Women (NCW) in New Delhi. Many other meetings were called by women's groups, such as MARG and the Lawyers Collective, to discuss the different drafts put forward by the NCW. The Special Cell also deposed to the joint parliamentary committee on the domestic violence bill.

Our research on Section 498A of the IPC in the police records was motivated by the very limited use the law had in the case of abused women. Women found that the only law on domestic violence had the effect of alienating them from their marriages and families, threatening their livelihoods, and leaving them to deal with disbelief and hostility from the police. This further distanced them from the formal justice system. Above all, society branded them as 'liars' and 'bad' women. The Special Cells were at the time handling more than 400 cases a year, of which only 0.4 per cent went to court. More than 80 per cent of the cases had to do with emotional and physical abuse in marriages and families. We had two questions: Why were the police unable to understand the pain of women, and what language were they using to convey it to the courts?

One thing was very clear—abused women wanted the violence in their marriages and families to end. However, this did not mean that they wanted their marriages and family relations to end. They needed assistance to challenge violence and help them rebuild their sense of self and dignity, while regaining the ability to earn and provide for themselves and their families. In our experience, most abused women actively resisted going to court, both criminal and civil. They perceived it as a 'final' step, and there was very little hope associated with it. It was considered a long, arduous and expensive process with an unknown outcome, which would not guarantee non-violence or a better quality of life. It seemed to them that they had more to lose than gain by going to court. The findings of our research confirmed these beliefs (Dave and Solanki 2000). Echoes of this were heard among women across the country, and this added to our resolve to actively campaign for the Protection of Women from Domestic Violence Act, which was to provide relief and protection from domestic violence on a speedy basis.

In the late 1990s, the Lawyers Collective's Indira Jaising rejoined the campaign for a law on domestic violence, and led it till the bill was passed by parliament in October 2005. She travelled across the country, met women's groups of different hues, as well as lawyers and scholars, to understand all aspects of the issue, keeping in mind the need for consensus building. I joined her on her New York leg of a study tour to the US, and it was exhilarating and enriching to participate with her in the preparatory work to build a robust legislation. What we learnt from this visit is reflected in the various mechanisms laid down in the act.

The Special Cells not only participated in the Lawyers Collective-led campaign and programmes for drawing up rules for the domestic violence act, but also advocated providing adequate infrastructural support and resources to the law. In particular, this related to preparing the departments of women and child development, and the law and judiciary to administer it in word and spirit. This was aided by us being resource persons for the training of judges and protection officers, and engaging in deep discussions for developing the content for a manual to be used by protection officers and service providers.

In 2007, the Special Cell was notified as a service provider by the Government of Maharashtra. So, in 20 years, the field action project was transformed into a state-funded programme. Its growth had been helped by a process of cross-fertilisation—while we planned changes, we were also open to new ideas and allowed room for influence. Participating in the simultaneous campaigns to address violence against women and domestic violence brought depth to both processes, enhancing our ability to respond to specific issues. When the Special Cells became a government programme, many more agencies and state governments were prompted to pay attention to the concept. They were included in the UNDP and central government-led Access to Justice project, and was invited to initiate Special Cells in Madhya Pradesh and Haryana in 2006.

The Government of Haryana took the Special Cell strategy seriously because it had been adopted by the Maharashtra government and recognised as a service provider under the Protection of Women from Domestic Violence Act. This was followed by the Oxfam inviting TISS to open Special Cells in four states—Orissa, Uttar Pradesh, Gujarat, and Andhra Pradesh. The Oxfam invitation was instigated by a graduate of TISS who had been a fieldwork student in the Special Cell, and convinced women's groups in Rajasthan to begin Special Cells there.

Our unique selling point was our approach to offering socio-legal services for violence against women, and demonstrating and replicating context-specific coordinated responses by engaging three government departments—home, women and child development, and the law and judiciary. The three areas simultaneously addressed were framing policy, formulating a programme to tackle violence against women, and preparing the law enforcement machinery to respond purposefully to violence against women and domestic violence. This meant working across the departments, and bringing them together on a common platform.

Working on violence against women from within the police system is still relevant, and we continue to experiment, struggle and learn. While we expanded and replicated Special Cell units in Maharashtra in about 18 months, we were persistently affected by the dynamics inside and outside the police organisation. The Special Cells bore the brunt of the ongoing power struggle between the Departments, services, and their conflicts of interest. TISS had promised to consolidate the work of the Special Cells and facilitate a smooth handover to the government. Only in 2007 did the heat die down, after the ACS (Home), in a monitoring committee meeting, took the position that the programme belonged to the state government and not to any one department.

A hard but necessary lesson that we learnt was that government administration was not a simple, easy, or straightforward matter. But the sustained badgering had the indirect effect of helping us fine-tune our interventions on women who had been subjected to violence. Burdened with questions, doubts and suspicions from one meeting to another, we were constantly arming ourselves with data, research and reasoning to counter the barriers raised by bureaucrats, the police, and other stakeholders, including women's organisations and groups. In 2009, the Mumbai High Court appointed an amicus curiae and a committee to look into a dowry death case and find preventive measures for violence against women. The Special Cell was a member of this committee. Following deliberations within it and the Special Cell deposing in the High Court, the department of women and child development promised the court that three Special Cells would be set up in every district of Maharashtra by 2012. This steady joining of the dots was necessary, however inefficient the process seemed.

Aftermath of Government Funding

Even after state government funding came in 2005, we were periodically reminded that the Special Cells were, in a way, still a field action project. This occurred mainly when we hit a resource crunch, monetary or otherwise, or when colleagues felt that those from TISS (including myself) were not participating in other activities. This was mostly when I was overwhelmed by the demands of administration or our social workers. Most field action projects of TISS had become independent organisations, and had been absorbed into other organisations, or into programmes supported by the government. The Special Cell had become a government-funded scheme, but TISS continued to play the roles of organiser and implementing agency. The Institute saw it both as an objective and as a mission, allowing faculty members to allocate up to 40 per cent of their time to it.

We at the Special Cells were relieved and very pleased at receiving the state's endorsement and financial support in 2005; however, these feelings did not last long. The battle between the government administration and the police, which almost vitiated 20 years of hard work and the healthy relationship we had built up with the force, saw to this. I was personally very keen to reduce the Institute's role in implementing the programme in Maharashtra. I wanted it to gradually hand over the programme to a collective—a registered society comprising social activists and professionals, representatives of academic and research institutions, and government officials from the relevant departments. This had also been a recommendation of the strategic management exercise.

This phase in the life of the Special Cells set in motion a whole new set of requirements—mechanisms, rules and capacity building—alongside the struggle to prevent the boat from capsizing. Although the Special Cells had been considered to be of value by the government and the police just months ago, new circulars were received every few weeks, which undermined the spirit of the workers, as well as their work. I saw this as the right time to put the erstwhile field action project into perspective, especially when the role and responsibility given to TISS meant that some police officers thought it had a 'say', while they seemed to be losing theirs. It has to be noted here that the important issue for them was not the Special Cells per se, but that of losing control over them.

While grappling with the demands of this situation, we were also being drawn on for training the police on violence against women in Maharashtra, social workers in Maharashtra and Rajasthan, and demonstrating how Special Cells functioned in Haryana and Madhya Pradesh. Thus, exhausted but charged with the possibilities, we allowed ourselves to plunge into initiating Special Cells in other states in late 2006. We recognised that we had gathered a wealth of experience on a variety of issues around the subject of violence against women. This had come from deep engagement with the abused women we dealt with, close interaction with the police and criminal justice systems, with communities, and with the women's movement. We had built our knowledge and skills for direct interventions in violence against women, training, research, and advocacy. Our experience of working with the police enabled us to answer questions on the systemic response to violence, on law and justice for abused women, and to encourage police personnel to carry on the battle against violence against women.

The demands on the Special Cells were steadily increasing. This was a time when the workers carried out the core work of the Special Cells, as well as organised programmes in the community to try to prevent violence against women. They also trained new social workers, updated police personnel on the subject, developed their own areas of interest, and did research on specific subjects like child abuse, communication with abused women, and socio-legal work in communities. This allowed for both individual and organisational growth, creating synergy for conceptualising practices and understanding and developing interventions to help women. Over the years, this group of social workers trained and developed teams across Maharashtra, Rajasthan, Madhya Pradesh, and Haryana. Skills specifically required to work with the criminal justice system were also learnt, and paid special attention to, so that they could help abused women to navigate it.

Stepping out of Mumbai and Maharashtra gave us the opportunity to test our understanding of responses and strategies to battle violence against women. We had to recognise and face different realities in different states and regions, and our strategies had to be modified to suit their socio-cultural environments. This meant being both discerning and perceptive, and understanding cultural nuances. Simultaneously, we had to deal with different stakeholders, both in governments and in the civil society, to build a consensus on responding to violence against women. The proposal that we presented to the Haryana government laid out why Special Cells were relevant, and emphasised the importance of institutionalising them and expanding the network (see Appendix 5). It did work out more or less that way, with the Haryana government dovetailing the Special Cells to the Protection of Women from Domestic Violence Act at a later date.

With the Act of 2005 recommending that protection officers, who preferably had a degree in social work, be appointed, the work of the Special Cells and its workers was validated and made visible in the law. Special Cells workers were asked to train protection officers in Maharashtra. Now, a programme to expand Special Cells to eight more states is underway, and the central government, along with multilateral and bilateral agencies, is encouraging the setting up of new Special Cells and looking to the functioning ones to support, nurture, and aid their understanding on responses to violence against women. The existing Special Cell teams have matured, and are now able to set in motion similar processes with like-minded bodies and groups, and develop skills and resources to combat violence against women.

The Resource Centre for Interventions

The Resource Centre for Interventions on Violence against Women was set up in 2008 to promote a consistent engagement with the issue of violence against women. It is to plan and initiate effective interventions with different stakeholders through training and modelling, and support research to enable a deeper understanding of the issue as well as the mediations possible. The Centre will also advocate structural changes, and create and strengthen organisations and their networks across the country to study and champion women's right to live with dignity. The Special Cells' mission statement and booklet on monitoring indicators largely define the scope of work of the resource centre.

The Centre's vision of capacity support involves creating a strong cadre of professionals and activists on violence against women, within the government and civil society institutions and organisations. It views the training of different stakeholders in interventions on violence against women as important, while building an understanding of the subject in state structures and systems. Developing trainers and training modules, mentoring individual workers and teams, and having resource persons at the centre to share, document, and study interventions on violence against women are part of the programme. The general effort is to build effective services, innovations and experiential learning, and demonstrate effective models to interested stakeholders. This includes developing region-specific services, strategies and interventions, while reviewing existing services for effectiveness and restructuring them while working towards institutionalisation. A major aim is to build up a consummate practice, and to be able to feed into policy, procedures, advocacy, and laws on violence against women.

At the time of the Centre's inception, the projects in the pipeline included supporting the Oxfam-funded Special Cells in Gujarat, Odisha, Uttar Pradesh, and Andhra Pradesh, although not all of them have materialised. We also had to initiate and support UNDP-funded Special Cells in seven states, besides training protection officers in Maharashtra. New social workers had to be inducted for the next stage of expansion in the state, while the Odisha police required training on working with violence against women. In addition, a model of work had to be developed for protection officers in the magistrates' courts in Mumbai.

The resource centre was located in the school of social work at TISS, and an attempt was made to incorporate all the lessons learnt by the Special Cells over the years in its structure. The existing Special Cells were considered one of its programmes, and the requests related to violence against women that came to them were routed through the Centre. Two persons with five to 10 years experience in interventions formed the core group at the centre, which gave Special Cell workers the space to contribute to strengthening institutional mechanisms and processes by drawing on their experience of directly working with abused women. To begin with, funds were to come from existing sources, and new persons were to be recruited according to the needs of the assignments taken up by the Centre. All the money coming in from assignments was to go into building a nest egg to sustain the work between projects and develop new ideas. The agencies that entrusted the Centre with assignments had to pay a fee, as well as bear all the costs associated with them.

Between 2009 and 2011, the Special Cells and the resource centre moved into many new areas of activity. In Maharashtra, the Special Cells were assigned the role of service provider, and one worker from each unit was given the additional role of protection officer to implement the Protection of Women from Domestic Violence Act. To mark the 25 years of work on violence against women by the Special Cells, open houses were organised for women and their families in the districts where they are located. In addition to women, the police and other individuals and organisations joined in celebrating the occasion. In 2009, to contribute towards developing a social work curriculum, a national conference on the theme of 'Conceptions of Interventions on Violence against Women' was organised at TISS for social work educators and Special Cell workers from all over the country.

Outside Maharashtra, in the same period, the resource centre worked along with Oxfam and local organisations towards setting up and institutionalising Special Cells in Gujarat, Odisha, Uttar Pradesh, and Andhra Pradesh. The Special Cell approach is now being demonstrated in five districts of Orissa and in four districts of erstwhile Andhra Pradesh. A dialogue has been initiated with the governments of Uttar Pradesh and Gujarat for the same purpose.

In Gujarat, the Special Cells have been institutionalised across districts as a joint programme of the Departments of Police and WCD, as a result of the RCI–VAW's advocacy.

Meanwhile, the Special Cells in Haryana and Delhi continue to go from strength to strength. Conducting research on the issue of violence against women and documenting the findings are an integral aspect of the work of the Centre. Capacity building among various stakeholders—such as social workers, counsellors, grass-roots workers, protection officers, the police, and judicial magistrates—are conducted on a continuous basis to enhance their ability to respond to violence against women. The Centre's projects have included research on the strategies of the Special Cells, a study on child marriage in Haryana, and a study on the implementation of the Protection of Women from Domestic Violence Act in four states.

The existing work with Special Cells approach and models in various states has translated over the past three years into new innovation practice for and with state departments for other forms of Violence against Women intervention systems. For example, design and training of personnel for Emergency Response Helplines for Women in Distress in Gujarat grew from the Special Cells engagement, and in itself gave rise to invitations from other state and non-state agencies. The RCI–VAW team itself has raised new resources to expand its own capacities to better repond to the rapidly expanding scope of work, to consolidate and carry forword policy and legal advocacy work with more state and non-state stakeholders in newer geographies on a wider scale, and to research, disseminate and publish.

Supporting Responses to Violence Against Women

The resource centre continues to provide support to organisations and initiatives that respond to violence against women. This takes the form of sharing data, training modules, procedural documents, and other papers and research, as well as setting up appointments to visit Special Cells and interact with their workers. At present, TISS is working with seven states to implement Special Cells effectively. The process of engaging with women, their communities, the criminal justice system, and society at large on the issue of violence against women continues to be the core work of the Special Cells and the resource centre.

The present team at the Centre is set to review its mandate to become more relevant to the ground realities of violence against women. It continues to engage with the state to find the resources required to scale up the quality of social services and sustain them, and to inform all stakeholders of the dynamics of intervention. Increasing the visibility of the work on violence against women, and the capacities of the Centre to manage the knowledge built over the past three decades, are also on the agenda. Different stakeholders have approached the resource centre to initiate Special Cells—students who did their fieldwork at a Special Cell, the police from different states, UN agencies, funding agencies, women's organisations, and the NCW. This has not only led to a dialogue with officials in various states, but also to the setting up of Special Cells, training personnel for them, and monitoring their performance. There has also been an association with state government schemes linked to the Protection of Women from Domestic Violence Act.

Our work on the ground, and networking and advocacy, have influenced some of the programmes in the Twelfth Five-Year Plan (2012–17), which aims to address violence against women in numerous ways. We envisage playing a further role in developing ideas to extend socio-legal support to abused women, and working on women's social and cultural rights, as well as their economic and political ones. But it has to be said that there are many hurdles in the way. For one, just convincing the home department, the criminal justice system, and the police that there is an enormous amount of violence against women and children is an uphill task. Weaving together the activities of the departments of home and women and child department to implement a coherent policy is another. At the same time, there is the real threat of the bureaucratisation of social services on one side, and the NGO-isation of state responsibilities on the other, while state services are still too few in number. Amidst this, changes in the criminal justice system are exceedingly slow.

At TISS, which we continue to rely on a great deal for institutional support, the Special Cells are still a project, but one that demands an amazing amount of work. In 2006, a member of the governing board of the institute asked, 'Why did the Special Cells not expand earlier? Why did it take 18 years?' My emphatic answer was,

> It takes time for the government and the courts to see any social service organisation's work. And to create even a ripple in the police, government, or criminal justice systems, the organisation's work has to have been visible for a long time. The minute one government took the lead and accepted us, many more followed suit.

I have narrated at great length what we did and why we did it through the years. But I feel it would not be fair to omit the critical observations made by women, women's groups, and the police on the Special Cells. A generic comment usually heard on our work is, 'Oh, domestic violence cases! You are not working on criminal cases, like rapes and caste violence?' Our route, charted by our objectives, can be seen as only working with individuals and offering them psychological help. Unfortunately, social work with individuals is not highly valued as 'development', or creating 'livelihoods' in the economic sense. 'Counselling is hardly a help,' they say.

In the evaluation study done in 2004, women's critique of the Special Cells was largely centred on us not using force against aggressors, or making sure the police gave women what they wanted. About 9 per cent of the women who had approached Special Cells and were not satisfied with its services offered such reasons.

Women's organisations' critique of the Special Cells has been different in different phases. They have ranged from 'crossed over to the state' or 'co-opted by the state' and 'working with the establishment', to 'Why should there be Special Cells? Women do not go to police stations, and the police are unresponsive to them.' There has also been criticism that we did not keep women's groups informed about our participation in government or high court committees. In the early years, there was tension because of differences in our approach to social work and what some women's organisation's believed the right response to abused women should be. For instance, we maintained that we had to be detached from our work to be effective, while women activists asked why we were not sheltering abused women in our homes if we were so concerned about them.

Criticism from the police came mostly during training sessions, occasions on which they were at their resistant best. A frequent question was, 'Has it reduced violence against women?' Then there were observations such as, 'For women, violence becomes an accepted part of marriage', and 'Urban areas are different from rural ones; try working there'. There was also ridicule of women's autonomy and self-determination, and they asked, 'What if a woman is in real danger?' and 'What can a social worker, who is only there between 10 AM and 6 PM, do when we are there 24 hours?' And of course, the trump card was, 'What about violence against men? What are you doing about that?'

I am not saying that all the criticism was unwarranted, because some of the observations made by stakeholders were of strategic interest. Yet, to my understanding, what matters most is the ability of feminist socio-legal services to leverage the power of women, the law, the police, and social systems to work against subjecting women to violence.

7

Pulling it Together: Reflections and the Learning

When I hear about the ongoing struggles and concerns of the special cells teams, I often ask myself why we should continue to engage with the state, and also read to find arguments for and against this. Seen from one angle, the state has been progressively distancing itself from the people and abdicating its responsibility towards them. I have read and heard from a variety of people why, in today's environment, it would be better to divorce ourselves from the state. In spite of all this, what resonates with me—and, I believe, with the Special Cells teams—is something that political and social activist Aruna Roy wrote in a daily,

> We must engage with the state and make it work for us. The state has the people's resources and they are only guardians of it, they do not own it; they have to work with people for public welfare, they have to be in it together (*The Times of India*, August 2011).

This argument sums up the reason why we continue to believe in our work. We have to engage with reality and demand that the governance system work for us. If, as Jeremy Cronin of the South African Communist Party puts it, democracy is speaking truth to power, making truth powerful, and the powerful truthful, we have to speak and engage as equals.

In the previous chapters, I attempted to build a context by charting the development of thought on the issue of violence against women; the organic growth of the Special Cells; and its present engagement with not only abused women, but also with society at large.

Figure 7.1: Context of the Special Cells

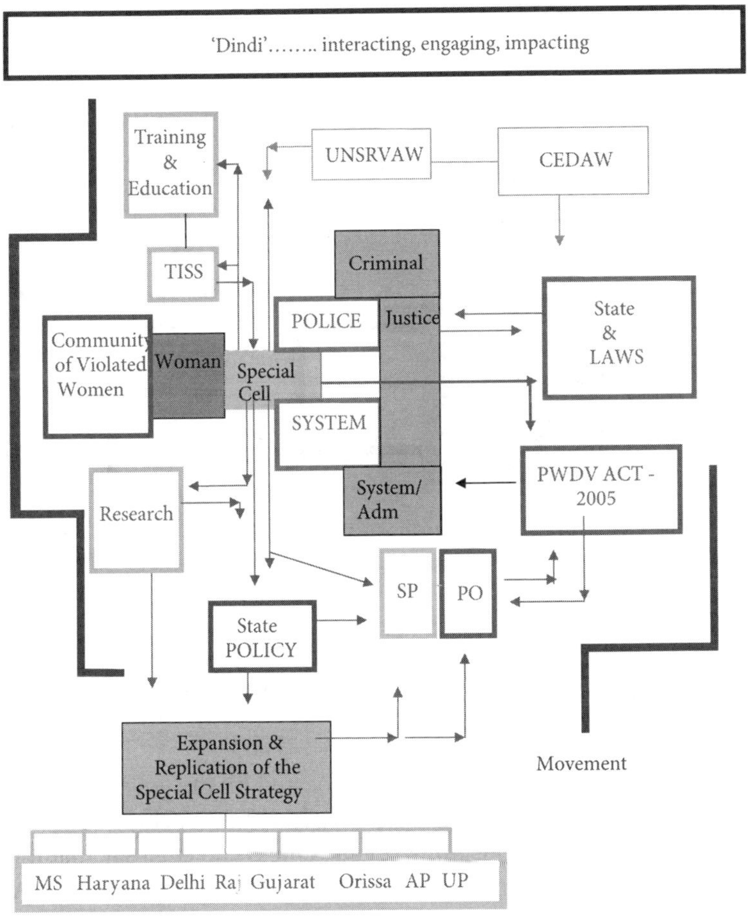

Here, I would like to examine the patterns that have emerged from the previous chapters. In learning from the Special Cells' engagement with violence against women, five interconnected themes stand out:

- The need to understand the nature of the state, the police, and governance when it comes to social work;
- The need for social work education and practice that is critical and political;
- The need for socio-legal work that deepens the roots of women's autonomy and promotes social justice;

- The need for webs of relationships to sustain individual and community well-being; and
- The need to develop a finer understanding of power, autonomy and agency.

Figure 7.2: Building an Argument

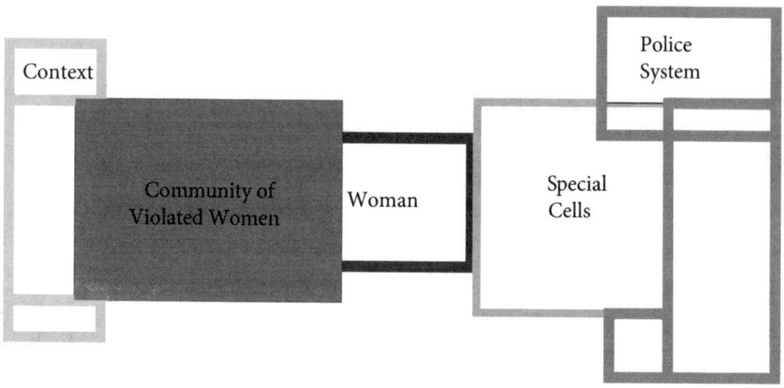

Understanding the Nature of the State, Police and Governance

Ensuring that adequate funds are allocated by the government to the social sector, in particular to social services such as those for abused women, is a constant struggle. One could even say that it is akin to extracting money from a person unwilling to part with it. At the same time, the state recognises that it has not delivered quality services. The pressure on it to perform makes it cajole NGOs into taking up public services, thereby transferring its responsibilities. Although it does not invest in resources, either social or physical, and pays personnel only an honorarium at best, it desires control over a programme's administration and its physical assets. In the world outside, India strikes the pose of being a self-sufficient country, which is not very poor, and refuses small aid. This has meant a decrease in aid for some social issues from international funding agencies, bilateral agencies, and from the government. While the state talks of private–public partnerships, it has a long way to go in learning what real partnerships are, let alone working as part of one. Civil servants in general do not want to work in the social sector, which seems to have very little value or importance in their concept of social justice, and in the scheme of governance.

Even as I write, the tussle with the state goes on. The state and its bureaucracy are very slow to adopt change—in their perceptions, ideology, attitudes, and approaches. A good example is the so-called counselling centres in police stations refusing to admit that battered women have been subjected to violence or crime. Decisions are taken without the participation of those who will be affected by them, and often, they are the last to know. Bureaucrats are usually confused about the structure and mechanisms of new services and approaches, such as the Special Cell. In the absence of a consistent vision, they may muddle through listening to different stakeholders, call meetings at short notice without agendas, and reinvent the wheel, ignoring history and context. They constantly tinker with schemes, their actions based on individual opinions and not on any reliable data or research. Even if there are supposedly logical explanations for reorganisation, they do not have the power, personnel, or budget to carry them out. Each incumbent comes with her/his own frame of reference, and pet theories about how things ought to be done. The net result is that social workers like us are forced to deal with ambiguity.

Power is central to everything—the state, the bureaucracy and the police. Everything is seen in terms of 'them' and 'us'. Apart from posturing, power and position are reflected in symbols—which chair you sit in, and which seat is occupied in a car or a jeep. Erasing history or not acknowledging it is also a function of power. The Special Cells challenged violence against women, questioning the power of the aggressors, their community, and their oppressive belief systems. It drew power from the law, morality and ethics. When the same understanding is extended to the state and its functionaries—essentially, when power is questioned—the result is threats and retaliation by removing the self from the action, while continuing to draw power from the position (Foucault 1995).

Command and control is the mantra of the police organisation, and this is increasingly experienced in all interactions with it. The police's need to control leads them to think and feel that they set the standard. Being a public service, they need not see themselves as social workers, but little conviction is seen in their work. This is especially the case when they say things like, 'The law will not change society, mindsets have to change', or when they marry off rape victims to rapists as a part of 'rehabilitation'. Different approaches, often location-driven, are visible in the police, where inter-departmental conflicts, tensions between service cadres, and territorial concerns are rife. The Special Cells use multiple lenses—social work, feminism and socio-legal approaches—to analyse and intervene in violence against women, but persuading the police to see things the same way has been a formidable task.

Emily Miles, a senior civil servant in the UK Home Office, who held a Winston Churchill Fellowship in 2010–11, undertook an exercise to understand the requirements of government and civil society collaborations. When she visited India in 2011, I was invited to share my experiences and thoughts on the Special Cells' strategic alliance with the police. Our interaction was interesting, and it allowed me to articulate the following points.

The environment was by and large favourable to the Special Cells innovating and demonstrating their services in the police system, an idea that was picked up by individual police officers and replicated in their next posting, sharing their infrastructure and administration with social workers. Although Ms Miles hoped for change in a system's culture with such partnerships and I appreciated the need for it, I had to point out that there were several factors involved in changing the culture of a system, and that we were just one of the many efforts required.

Among these efforts, one was that the government had to collaborate with people's organisations on public policies and services. To work together, it had to intrinsically respect people, and their dignity and value, and each interaction, process, or mechanism had to reflect this. A smooth partnership exists only when the government or a civil society organisation does not flex its muscles overtly, although each is aware of the other's power and continues working towards equalising it. Exercising restraint for a common purpose and recognising interdependence are what translate into a strategic alliance.

Resources and funds from the government for public services are perceived as dependence on the state. At the same time, it is debatable whether private-sector donations can be seen as participation by citizens or the community. While they may be able to supplement what the state provides, they cannot be a substitute, especially on issues such as violence against women, where the ideology of the community itself supports and perpetuates violence against women.

We need to address the real issues in inter-departmental work, and rethink and redefine our priorities and agendas to meet the needs of the complex realities of our times. Setting up a national mission for the empowerment of women to bring about a convergence of state resources and services would be in line with this. The government, and in particular the police, need to work with civil society groups for public services to be effective. A DGP once asked, 'Why should I give space in my house (the police station) to an NGO to work on violence against women?' He was only echoing what goes through the minds of bureaucrats and policemen all over the country—I will not share 'my' space or resources with 'outsiders'. The answer to him was, 'A police station is a public space, not any one person's house or property.' A strategic alliance always has a distinct purpose, and some of the tensions that exist are due to mechanisms of monitoring and accountability that are not consistent or clearly spelt out, as they should be if governance is to be effective.

My conviction is that change comes from within, and I do not mean this in a philosophical sense. Conditions for the transformation of the self and systems exist (Nussbaum and Sen 1993), and the human spirit continuously resists oppression, struggling to be humane (Freire 1972). Some individual policemen in the system, whatever their position, location, or power, were consistent in their efforts to open their minds and the doors of the system to us. Such officers were instrumental in the Special Cells taking root and growing. Similarly, some bureaucrats were attentive and used their network to overcome obstacles, enabling the progress of the Special Cells. Many of the policemen on the ground have been of enormous support to the work on violence against women.

Every time there has been active resistance from individuals in power or a lobby, there has been a proverbial silver lining in the cloud. This will hopefully continue till all individuals and systems are on par, and democracy delivers on its promise. My social work education, its context and training make me repose faith in human beings and their spirit, sometimes even to the extent of discounting the actions of patriarchal individuals and systems.

Social Work Education and Practice

A teacher once said to me that social work means being a highly conscious person, for it entails praxis, or the use of knowledge. Reading Freire and practising his principles have sharpened my understanding of education and social work, and instilled in me the realisation that social work education and practice has to be both critical and political.

Building and nurturing relationships are crucial to people-centred work. We spent a lot of time and effort in establishing relationships with people in the police system and the bureaucracy, with women and their families, with communities, and with the women's movement. We read, interacted and observed to understand our constituency, since social work is engaging with people in the quest for social justice. Social work is working on the fine details, helping to weave an intricate web of support for people to lead wholesome and fulfilling lives. It also involves building an appreciation of its need in social workers, providing them with support in their day-to-day work, and encouraging them to uphold human values.

Simultaneity is another pillar of the social work process, and needs to be a key component in social work education. It is the sense or awareness of it all happening at the same time that creates so many moments in which the penny drops, providing fresh insights into myriad people and situations. Living and interacting with multiple ideologies, political thoughts, hierarchies, religions, and races help to build and sustain a pluralistic and syncretic orientation. Social work is also a long-term commitment to building, dismantling, or reconstructing individual lives and social structures. The simultaneity of working with social structures, systems and individuals means that every shift and change in any one of them organically alters the nature of all three. The cascading nature of this can have far-reaching consequences.

Social work believes that the demarcations between a social worker's personal and professional identities blur over a period of time. The values one learns gradually co-exist as practice in one's private and public lives. The passion, conviction and commitment I brought to helping abused women lead dignified lives aided me in reaching this goal. My understanding of social work rests within the context of people trained to provide people-centred and humane services. This has little to do with so-called professionalism, and all the hierarchy, efficiency and expertise that it entails.

Violence is corrosive, intellectually and emotionally, and healing its effects may require socio-legal services; however, the starting point is human interaction, both verbal and non-verbal. A smile, a touch, a hug, or a tear precipitate the first tentative but giant step for an abused woman and a social worker.

Socio-legal Work and the Struggle for Social Justice

Having a long-term vision is rare, but it is very useful if structures or institutions have to be built to articulate that vision. My experience has been that the desire for a just world propels you into opening your mind to different influences, including even a change in your idea of what is just. I consider the Special Cells a part of the mission to end violence against women. It defined its work on violence against women, and participated with other stakeholders in a wide variety of activities, debates and struggles without losing sight of its stated purpose—bringing relief to the abused woman, a human being.

A colleague once remarked, 'Your politics of intervention has led us to do the *tandava nritya* (dance that celebrates the cycle of creation, preservation and dissolution).' Yes, we created spaces for violence against women in the police and the government by systematically engaging them to respond to the issue. While this resulted in some milestones, we also had to deal with periodic tremors, including power struggles and turf wars, while holding on to the values of self-respect, self-worth, and the dignity of social work principles. The support we received from communities of women, women's organisations, and other friends was what saw us through.

In our mission, we were introduced to a wide range of thoughts, beliefs, ideologies, and approaches. Apart from reading, we were involved in various activities and discussions to fathom the reality of women's situations. No one theoretical formulation could explain the complex dimensions that I, as a social worker, faced. No one theory fitted the experiences of all the women who had been made helpless, and those of our workers. Our study of violence against women challenged our thinking and our beliefs. I learnt that all the answers were not to be found in books or theories, whose purpose was only to aid you in finding explanations.

The concepts of preventive, curative and remedial work were clear in theory, and understood by me. If there was a hierarchy within, then preventive work was the best. The complex interplay of oppressive social structures and institutions, and the responses required were learnt from every woman who came to the Special Cells. This redefined concepts like 'prevention' in a more real way. I came to realise that the law did not mean only going to court, and that socio-legal work was preventive as much as it was curative and remedial. With almost every woman, our work was all three—preventive, curative and remedial.

Social change, or a shift in the thinking of societies and communities, is a slow process. With the law censuring violence against women, there is a chance that all women may not readily accept family violence as a fact of life; however, it is doubtful whether community institutions will support this. What we require are services outside these spaces, and these services have in turn to be in strategic locations, with the potential to act as agents of change. Community institutions and kinship ties are no longer able to respond to the needs and wants of its members. Their capacities are unable to match the rapid and unfamiliar changes taking place around them, due to increased mobility, loosening ties, and a lack of control over resources. Alongside this, state institutions and systems have only a limited reach and role in addressing social and cultural changes.

Globalisation has had an inadequate effect on breaking down caste and class barriers, and its impact has sometimes even been the other way round. Pockets of economic growth, higher education and urban employment amid a decreasing influence of the family and local community result in young people without a strong base of intellectual, emotional, or material resources. While social barriers are being lowered as guided by the Constitution, this co-exists with feudal values. The space for the articulation of rights has widened, but this co-exists with contention over all rights. In this scenario, an inclusive ideology, incisive social analyses, and committed social workers are critical to the struggle for social justice.

This is borne out by data on the increasing number of women reaching out for socio-legal services from the Special Cells. Traditionally, social services have been offered by the 'haves', often in a benign and good-intentioned way, but also patronisingly. Such services have been few and far between, and their focus is mainly on groups defined as poor or piteous by religion or popular culture. These services are embedded in the socio-economic and political understanding of the giver. The Indian socialist republic is expected to move beyond narrow schools of thought, and aspire to be a pluralistic society that respects every citizen's right to substantive equality in the eyes of the Constitution and the law. But the problem is that it has left citizens behind to struggle for their rights. In the past 50 years, the state's ability to provide for the welfare and well-being of its people has come under severe stress, and the effectiveness of governance is now at an all-time low. Social services cannot be a bureaucratic appendage of the state if quality and standards are to be maintained, while remaining humane. They have to be led by constant innovations, research and leaps of imagination. They cannot be run by the government alone, although core services need to be fully funded, and service providers have to be able to participate in policymaking and monitoring.

The three strands interwoven on the ground for effective work by the Special Cells were: upholding women's dignity, self-respect and self-worth; harnessing state resources to help provide social justice and ensuring that the state adhered to its obligations; and sticking to democratic values and processes in day-to-day work. One of the ways to engage with the state was through negotiation. Social work education had taught me to work with people, but negotiation skills were not a part of it. This was acquired on the job. What seems simple and logical to you could be the opposite to another set of people.

For example, a senior police officer wanted to know why the Special Cells did not submit a monthly report on the number of 'cases disposed'. What was the problem with 'closing' files at the Special Cells? The problem, as perceived by him, was that the Special Cells were not maintaining data that would indicate the quantum of work done. Listening to this, recognising the assumption, and then explaining the Special Cells' perspective in a language understandable to the police called for negotiation skills of a high order. We also had to convince the officer that keeping files open was in accordance with our practice of feminist social work, that we maintained proper records, and could even provide data for indigenous research. Negotiations meant leveraging experience, knowledge of the subject and the system, and discipline and pluralistic values.

Engaging with the criminal justice system in particular required us to think on our feet, holding on to the core values of our work while not being cowed down by the covert but unmistakable presence of coercive power. We had to learn to work with confidence and authority, even at the risk of being considered assertive or aggressive. This also meant that we could accommodate people with our kind of values, but that it was difficult to make room for others. Since a large part of the work with women relies on verbal communication, we laid emphasis on paying attention to the language they used to share 'their plight'. This also taught us to organise our thoughts, and think more clearly about the issue of violence over time. Similarly, communicating with the criminal justice system meant that we had to learn its grammar and language.

What have I learnt? What were the key reasons for the Special Cells' effectiveness? Looking back, I would say self-discipline, a women-centred ideology, deriving strength from the determination of women and sharing it with them, and treating everybody, especially women, with respect. The fight to break the cycle of poverty and the violence it produces and reproduces is long and exhausting. There are no short cuts. What helps is a consciousness of the use and abuse of power by individuals and the social structure, and of the need to adhere to democratic values. To me, social work has been a critical education and an ongoing dialogue, raising my awareness and making me look for explanations for all the whys and the whats. Thus, what began as an experiment led to the creation of an approach and a service; the reach of this service has increased manifold; resources have been raised from the state to work on violence against women; we can offer trained personnel to work on it; and inroads have been made into institutions such as the police system and the law.

Figure 7.3: Dynamic Socio-legal Intervention

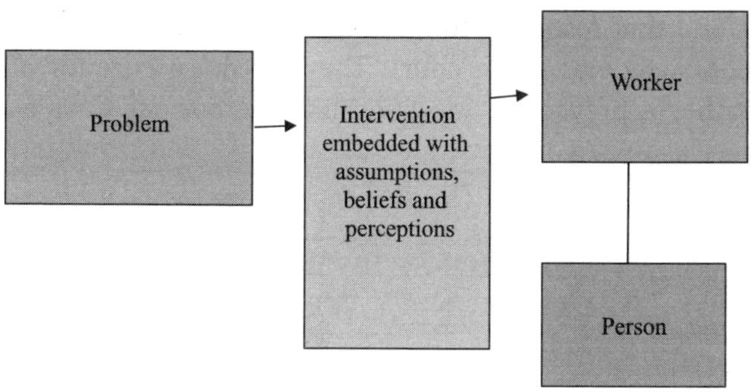

When I look at theories to explain the ideology of the work done by the Special Cells, I realise that it has been the application of a set of evolving beliefs, which has been shaped into responses to violence against women. You are presented with a problem, and you intervene in it on the basis of your understanding, and your assumptions and beliefs. The intervention in turn adds to your understanding of the problem, and that of the worker and the person involved. The dynamic interaction of these four broad units is governed by a range of influences and schools of thoughts. At the Special Cells, the work of trained personnel at the individual and the structural level—the police system—has been within a feminist social work paradigm on violence against women. This has been decisive in developing socio-legal interventions to stop violence against women.

Special Cell workers are free to pick issues that intrigue them and cultivate an interest in it. For example, work with men has developed as a distinct area because of the ideas that some members of the team had, and it has been included in the resource centre's range of activities. Yet, what is of value in the non-hierarchical organisation is the fact that everybody feels a sense of ownership over its work.

With regard to the question about what the Special Cells and its socio-legal services should aspire to, my answer is that they have to strive to deepen the roots of women's autonomy and social justice. They have to continuously understand the changing contours of society, the reasons for these, and the issues that need laws for remedial action. It has to be realised that laws are guides to manoeuvre through societal norms and expectations, and that resorting to them does not mean that cases have to necessarily end up in court. They are not a cure for all ills, but rather a preventive measure, like the Special Cells are for violence against women.

Webs of Relationships in Individual and Community Well-being

One of the interesting realisations has been the centrality of relationships. At the Special Cells, we have been forging, sustaining and expanding relationships all these years. Relationships, and their quality and value, affect your private and public lives. As a person, the influence of relationships on me has been profound—from my grandparents, parents and teachers, to colleagues and friends. Relationships deepen our experiences, shape our selves, and define our place in the community.

TISS, and the physical and mental space it provided, went a long way in drawing me and many others into webs of relationships. My first few steps towards building a relationship with the women's movement were taken while attending the second IAWS conference in Kerala, just before starting the Special Cell. In addition, being the secretary of Swadhar, I had interacted with the socialist leader Mrinal Gore, and had of course been introduced to women's issues by Professor Apte.

I have learnt that relationships are enriched and sustained if those involved can lucidly articulate their thoughts and values, and interpret both verbal and non-verbal signals. Reading the emotional content beneath what is stated rationally is often vital to effective communication. This is especially relevant in the Special Cells, where distraught women come with grievances of many kinds. Viewed from another angle, it is women's belief in relationships that brings them to the Special Cells, and it is relationships that motivate and inspire us to doggedly carry on with our work.

This brings me to the first few years of the Special Cell, when we were introduced to seemingly strange ways, norms and situations. My conscious and unconscious efforts to not be fazed by these led to some hilarious situations, but they also paved the way for good relations. Police officers in general adopt a style that projects the importance of their position in the hierarchy. In trying to not be overwhelmed by it, I attempted to stay aloof from the customary norms that policemen followed. I was once in a DCP (HQ)'s room for his signature and stood waiting for him to finish a phone call. Every time I leaned forward to point to the contents of the paper I had, we were interrupted by a bell ringing and several constables rushing into the room. This happened at least three times, and the DCP (HQ) kept asking me to sit down, which I did not. Finally, a bit reluctantly, he said, 'Ah, Anjali, you are pressing the bell on your side of the table.' In leaning forward, I had been ringing the bell, which brought policemen scurrying into the room. On another occasion, as was 'normal' to me, I was talking with my hands, and this sent a pen I was holding flying across the room. I had to try hard to keep the conversation going, while nonchalantly walking across the room and picking up the pen.

Then there was the time when I was invited to a breakfast meeting the CP had with the city's DCPs. I was the second person to be served since I was the only 'lady' at a table of 20 men. The police always believe that 'important' persons visiting them should be well hosted. The then Addl CP used to share cashew nuts with us social workers to serve Profesoor Apte when she visited us. The police, officers and constables, were also careful not to crack jokes in our hearing that would 'hurt our sentiments'. All this care and concern while introducing us to their ways contributed to initiating relationships that stood us in good stead, and built our confidence in the police system and in ourselves.

Pondering over it, I realise that my way of doing things has been thinking my way through an issue or a problem, and trying to make connections. I gather cues all the time and try to make sense of them in my context. I have always enjoyed listening to stories and watching the world go by, and I enjoy people and love them, quirks and all. So I continue to learn, often intuitively. For instance, liking the changes in students as time went by made me ready for change myself.

An important influence on my orientation was Professor Apte, who taught me as the project coordinator, and then the project director. The time I spent away from the Special Cell and the Institute gave me the opportunity to interact with a wider audience, often resulting in fruitful and lasting relationships. In 1993, my inclusion in the gender planning training project organised by the Department of Personnel and Training, Ministry of Human Resource Development, brought me in touch with Professor Naila Kabeer of the Gender Institute, London School of Economics and Political Science, UK. She was then with the Institute of Development Studies, Sussex. This was my introduction to the Gender Relations Framework, which provided a rigorous tool of analysis that allowed me to weave my experience and understanding into it. It became a mainstay of the training programmes that we developed for the police, the social workers, and other stakeholders on violence against women, and the Special Cells use it till date. Being part of the gender planning training project also made me aware of what gender studies was doing internationally.

Developing a Better Understanding of Power, Autonomy and Agency

Working at the Special Cells with individuals and systems, both at the same time, gave us the unique opportunity to understand various aspects of both, their influence on each other, and our position as a mitigating agency. There were the use and abuse of power; the power of individuals, social structures and institutions; the power of socialisation; the power of relationships; and relationships of power and powerlessness. We had to find our way through this maze to increase the autonomy and agency of women, so that they could stand up to violence. It had to be recognised that this process was political, and that made the change we desired that much harder to achieve.

Figure 7.4: Understanding Power, Autonomy and Agency

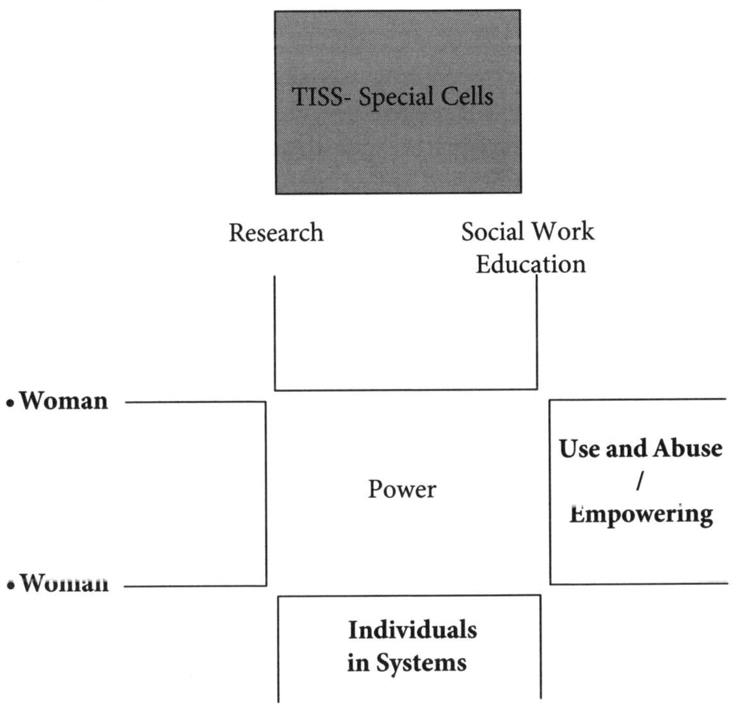

There are some women who are able to use their agency to say no to violence, seek help, and work hard to regain control over their lives. But this is not a given—every woman who is abused does not think of seeking help, or she either cannot or will not look for assistance. The Special Cells are located in the police system to draw on the power of the law and the Constitution to aid abused women to rebuild their lives, but this power is neither benign nor apolitical. I see feminist social work as the ideology that guides the mechanism by explaining why we need to engage with the state, and the spaces we need to create if we assume that the state is for the welfare of the people. If the state does not look out for its people, one of the ways of getting it to do so is by harnessing its resources, which actually belong to the people.

The label of 'social scientist from TISS' was useful to me, in that the academic institution provided me with a degree of power and credibility, enabling me to uphold its values and withstand day-to-day pressures. The institutional support was critical to studying and researching the social phenomenon of violence against women, and in getting systems to respond to the needs of women. The Special Cells were, in many ways, empowered by their association with TISS. And they in turn improved the comprehension of individuals, communities and the state through their work with women who had been ill-treated for long by their partners.

The language that victims and survivors use is different, and it helps women to retain their agency. The power of the word, I discovered, was important in lifting women from their experience of pain and misery, and getting them to recognise their ability to survive. It could also give them the will to pick up the pieces and put the past behind them. Just think of verbal abuse, the power that words have to cause hurt and even violence, and you recognise that it works in the other way as well. In the early days of the Special Cell, I remember using language to clearly understand the perspective of a woman who was hoping for reconciliation with her abusive and alcoholic husband. I asked if she wanted to go to her husband because she was married to him, or because she liked him as a person. Her shy but prompt reply was, 'I like him.' For me, the exchange threw fresh light on the issue, and for her, it threw fresh light on her motivation.

I perceive power as central to my attempt to explain the journey of the Special Cells. In my concept of the term, power is also agency. Autonomy is neutral; only in the context of a relationship does it come alive. Each has its own value and strength, and they interact with each other. Women, as human beings, have rights and agency, although a variety of factors may hinder their power to exercise them. The Special Cells have leveraged various sources of power, including the worker's individual power to work on violence against women, to make women realise they have autonomy and agency, and to put them to good use. In this journey, struggle and resistance have been an accompanying strand. Since the work we do changes power relations, it is political, and opposition to this is strong, all round.

Timeline of the Special Cell

1984: Begins functioning in the Commissioner of Police Office, Mumbai

1985: Begins training police on violence against women and children. CP, Mumbai, sends a proposal for funding the Special Cell to the Government of Maharashtra

1986: Becomes a member of the dowry committee, chaired by the Addl CP (Crime)

1987: Initiates Project Help at Sion Hospital to assist victims of bride burning. Organises national seminar on violence against women with the support of the union ministry of human resource development

1988: Opens Special Cell in Dadar police station, Mumbai

1990: Initiates regional and district-level training on violence against women with the police, supported by the union ministry of women and child development

1993: Becomes a member of the Maharashtra team on the gender planning training project, supported by the British Council and the central department of personnel and training. Professor M. Apte attends the Vienna UN Summit on Violence against Women. The DGP of Maharashtra sets up a committee to consider a cadre of social workers in the criminal justice system

1994: Opens Special Cell in Kandivali police station

1995: CP, Mumbai, sends a proposal for funding the Special Cell to the government of Maharashtra

1997: Completes research study on child sexual abuse. Completes 'Because the Personal is Political', a research study on Special Cells. Becomes an invited member of the state-level task force on violence against women

1999: Completes 'Shades of Courage', a research study on Section 498A, IPC

2000: Completes 'Journey from Violence to Crime', a three-part research study. Initiates the Centre for Research on Violence against Women

2001: UNIFEM, TISS, and the Government of Maharashtra sign a memorandum of understanding, making the Special Cell a joint programme of all three and with an agenda to expand across the state

Opens Special Cells in Ulhasnagar and Dombivali, supported by the UNFPA

2002: Sets up Special Cells in Navi Mumbai, Pune, Yavatmal, and Aurangabad. Introduces Special Cells in Jaipur, Rajasthan, and in Hyderabad, Andhra Pradesh

2003: Sets up Special Cells in Nashik, Wardha and Nanded

2005: The Department of Women and Child Development, Government of Maharashtra, takes over the Special Cell programme

The Parliament passes the Protection of Women from Domestic Violence Act

2006: The UNDP and the central government approach the Special Cell and TISS to replicate the process in Madhya Pradesh and Haryana

2007: Special Cells open in districts of Dhar, Madhya Pradesh, and Ambala and Jind, Haryana. Special Cells expand to 20 districts in Maharashtra

2008: Special Cells becomes a programme of the Government of Haryana

Sets up Resource Centre on Interventions on Violence against Women

2009: Completes 25 years

Initiates Special Cells in New Delhi at the behest of the Delhi Police and the National Commission for Women

Demonstrates Special Cells in Andhra Pradesh, Uttar Pradesh, Gujarat, and Odisha, with funding from Oxfam India

2010: Special Cells becomes a programme of the Government of Rajasthan.

Appendix 1

Tata Institute of Social Sciences Proposal to the Commissioner of Police, Mumbai

No.14211/ 954 /84 18.5.1984

Shri Ribero
Commissioner of Police
Bombay

Dear Sir:

Further to your talk on the report on undertrials with Dr. A.S. Desai, our Director, we would like to approach you to kindly consider the following project:

I had met you on March 8th in your office to discuss social work collaboration in the Social Service Cell of the Bombay City Police.

Today, an increased number of atrocities, committed against women and children, are coming to light. Gradually, we are discovering violence in the family itself and the treatment of women and children in the family. There are a variety of reasons for this violence which is taking place and needs to be attended. Communal violence is another threat to the displacement and ill treatment of women.

Many of these complaints reach the Police. The City Police of Bombay has made special efforts in creating a cell for complaints pertaining to the family. We feel that it would give greater mileage if a social worker is involved full-time with the cell, so that professional social service could be made available to such families.

<u>Our objectives for placing a worker</u>

1. Review the kind of complaints received and entertained in the last two years at the Social Service Cell. This would give us an idea as to the nature of work involved, and the strategy of work to be evolved.

2. Offer immediate services:

   a) Placement in institutions or referral to family agencies

   b) Financial Assistance

   c) Legal Aid

   d) Medical and Psychiatric treatment

   e) Other types of referrals.

..2/-

2

3. Be a liaison between the Police Office and organisation for women and children.

4. Create awareness amongst women themselves, among professional groups and the general public of the humiliations and atrocities particularly against women and children.

Duration of the Project

We visualise this project as an experimental project for about 5 years for us to mutually explore further avenues for better service.

Funds

While the project is on an experimental basis, funds will be mobilised by us from various funding organisations.

Operation

Work will begin with two trained social workers who will regularly sit in the Social Service Cell, Police Commissioner's Office. To fulfil the above objectives, the workers would pay home visits and contact collaterals and other agencies with regard to the clients and client system. The workers would be referred cases of family and personal psycho-social disturbances. Initially, the workers would orient themselves to the set-up of the Bombay City Police, simultaneously explaining their role to their colleagues. Visits to other police stations, lock ups, meeting officials of these situations, and their feedback on the way in which the work could be co-ordinated, would be the major aim.

Physical Set-up

The workers would require a table, a chair and a cupboard each. The space allotted to them would be in the social service cell. The place must have certain amount of privacy (probably partition) to deal with clients who need the assurance of confidentiality.

Administration and Transport

All administrative help like stationary, typing and other clerical work would be provided by the social service cell of the Bombay City Police. Transport or transport allowance, for official work, if and when necessary, could also be provided to the workers to make the operations smoother.

This is a brief outline of the work we visualise at the offices of Bombay City Police.

...3/-

3

We hope you will give us the opportunity to pave the way for a collaborative service between the police and for financial social work. Today, there is a growing awareness in society, and among women themselves, of the humiliations from which they suffer. To realise their efforts at being fully contributing members of society, they need our full support. We also accept the need for voluntary organisations to join hands with Government agencies to reach out to people in need.

On hearing from your office, we shall be happy to come and see you to discuss further details with you and your colleagues.

Thanking you and with warm regards,

Yours sincerely,

Meenakshi Apte

Mrs. M.J. Apte
Head, Dept. of Family and
Child Welfare

ls/

Appendix 2

The Commissioner of Police's Authority Letter

Office of the
Commissioner of Police,
Greater Bombay,
November 5, 1984.

A U T H O R I T Y L E T T E R

Ms. Anjali Dave has been deputed by the Tata Institute of Social Sciences, Bombay. to work in the Special Cell set up by the Greater Bombay Police to help Women in Distress. In cases of distress, harassment over dowry, physical and mental violence, etc. she would give assistance by way of legal aid, family assistance, etc. to women and children including those in lock-ups.

I hereby authorise Ms. Anjali Dave to visit Police Stations, Lock-ups and other Police offices of Greater Bombay Police Force to collect information.

I request the Judiciary, other Govt. departments and Institutions which cater to the needs of the above mentioned category of women and children to extend necessary co-operation to her.

12/11/84

(J.F.Ribeiro)
Commissioner of Police,
Greater Bombay.

COMMISSIONER OF POLICE
GREATER BOMBAY

Appendix 3

The Commissioner of Police's Letter of Acceptance to the Director, Tata Institute of Social Sciences

[illegible] [Spl.–G. B. P. 145 e.
G. L., H. D., No. 5817-D dated 15-2-24.]

No. 1140 / C.P./P.A. of 19

OFFICE OF THE COMMISSIONER OF POLICE

BOMBAY, 19-6-1984

FROM

THE COMMISSIONER OF POLICE,
GREATER BOMBAY.

To

The Director,
Tata Institute of Social Sciences,
Sion-Trombay Road,
Deonar, Bombay-400 088.

Dear Sir,

With reference to your two notes on the project to help women in distress reported at Police Lock-ups and the Police Commissioners Office I am grateful to you for the help offered. It will help this department to come to grips with the problems faced by helpless women whose present status in society exposes them to various forms of hardships. With the help of your Professor Smt. Meenakshi Apte and Kumari Anjali Dave and others I hope to offer some relief to these helpless women.

I have discussed with Smt.Apte and Kumari Dave when officers of the JAPU and Social Security Branch of the C.I.D. were present. The details had been worked out and we hope to start our work on Ist July on an experimental basis for three years in the first instance. Arrangements for accommodation and transport as possible will be made by us. Necessary instructions will be given to all Police Stations in Bombay City to afford all facilities to the workers appointed by the Tata Institute of Social Sciences for this project.

Yours faithfully,

(J.F.Ribeiro)
Commissioner of Police,
Greater Bombay.

Copy forwarded to Smt.Meenakshi Apte, Head, Department of Family and Child Welfare, Tata Institute of Social Sciences, Sion-Trombay Road, Deonar, Bombay-400 088.

Appendix 4

Thoughts Relevant to the Organisation and Administration of the Special Cell

In 2000, the Commissioner of Police (CP) in Nagpur requested us to support the school of social work there to set up a Special Cell in the city. This was Mr T. Singarvel, who had been the DCP (HQ) when the Special Cell was set up in Mumbai. We sent them these 'Thoughts Relevant to the Organisation and Administration of the Special Cell', which was drafted to help set up Special Cell units in the state.

Office and Working

- Each Special Cell is to have at least two workers, preferably a man and a woman, and not an all-male team.
- The Special Cell is responsible and accountable to the CP. For specific jobs, the CP refers the Special Cell to different DCPs, for instance, those in charge of crime, administration, and so on. If the CP feels that we should have someone to go to on a day-to-day basis, it will be the head of the Crime Branch (Prevention) or the DCP (HQ).
- The first Special Cell was set up at the CP's office, and the next two at police stations. At the police station, the Special Cell is accountable to the Senior Inspector, since he is the administrative head of the unit.
- Three monthly meetings are held with the CP, giving her/him brief reports of the work done, the highlights, the administrative clearances required, and future plans.
- The Special Cell is to be considered an independent unit, and therefore physical location is important. It has to be given an independent space, and this is worth asking for. This place should have easy public access, since police rules constantly change for security reasons, especially at the CP's office.

- All administrative and infrastructure support is to be given by the police, that is, furniture (tables, chairs, cupboards, and benches); stationery (paper, telephone diaries, envelopes, typewriter, typing material, and postage); infrastructure (telephone, fans, jeep for visits); and access to make STD calls, to the fax, and the wireless.
- An authority letter from the CP, granting permission to visit police stations, look at records, and visit lock-ups.

Organisation and Approach

- There has to be direct and easy access to the CP.
- The Special Cell should be allowed to evolve, and not be expected to frame rules immediately.
- Visit all police stations in Nagpur to introduce the Special Cell and its objectives. Joint efforts and the supplementary support role of the Special Cell are to be stressed.
- Maintain a distinct identity as social workers and keep in mind the boundaries while working with abused women.
- If possible, gradually get involved with other social projects of the police.
- At all times, a 'we-are-all-citizens-of-this-country' mode helps to ask questions, seek clarifications, and get information. The Special Cell can be considered a Special Officer under the Bombay Police Act, but we do not have any direct legal status, apart from the authority letter.

Scope of the Special Cell

- Dealing with any situation where a woman sees herself as abused, violated, or distressed, which creates anxiety, stress, or fear in her.
- The training of grassroots workers, women's groups, schoolchildren, college students, and the police on the issue of violence against women and children.

- Research, both agency-based projects and larger ones, related to violence against women.
- Networking with women's organisations, development organisations, and government agencies and departments, essentially to give and receive support, and to create a forum to discuss violence against women.
- Initiating programmes and projects as and when required.

METHODOLOGY

- Receiving applications for assistance.
- Maintaining an intake register.
- Registering women for referrals to other organisations, especially to lawyers.
- Working at the individual and at the group level with panchayats, parishads, and local committees.
- Maintaining a regular correspondence with police officers.
- It is very important not to become direct actors in the cases dealt with. Do not be a witness in any legal proceeding or give statements to the police. The Special Cell has to be independent of these processes, especially since we have no legal status.
- Records have to be maintained, although they pose practical difficulties. A detailed intake register, with pages on which to write down the highlights of each case, is helpful. Applications that are detailed are also helpful in documentation.
- The Special Cell, Mumbai, has documented the past 10 years of its work. We maintain a 'Yearly Diary of Events'. An annual report is advisable.

Appendix 5

Extracts from Project Proposal to the Government of Haryana

From the Introduction

The Special Cell is a social service provided to abused women by trained social workers located in the police system, with a clear understanding that violence against women is a crime and that it is the responsibility of the state to prevent and counter it. Hence its strategic location. Integrating social services with the police system can lead to a more coordinated, coherent, and in-depth response to the issue.

Strategic alliances between the state and the civil society to combat and respond to violence against women are considered an effective strategy by the UN Declaration on the Elimination of Violence against Women (1993). Over the last 22 years, the Special Cell in Bombay has established an effective mechanism to respond to violence against women, especially domestic violence. It has been incorporated within the state machinery slowly but surely, creating attitudinal shifts in it. The future of the Special Cells depends on how effectively these strengths and achievements can be built upon.

From Groundwork for the Special Cells in Haryana

Presentations and meetings were held with various state departments, and discussions on the relationship between the state, the police, communities, local government, and service providers on violence against women led to a recognition of the need for a mechanism like the Special Cells. For continued support and funding, it is necessary to house the Special Cells in a state department that can nurture its goals. It is important for all stakeholders to agree on their structure, location, ownership, and funding, since violence against women requires a multi-agency approach.

From Case for Institutionalising and Expanding the Special Cells in Haryana

Institutionalisation in a bureaucratic set-up is a long-term task and needs willingness on the part of the state machinery to assume ownership of the Special Cells, and a commitment at the senior-most levels of the police. In Haryana, a presentation made on the Special Cells was attended by senior officials, who were appreciative and supportive of the service. Also, the responses received from women, the police, and government officials have essentially acknowledged the need for this mechanism.

The primary goal of setting up Special Cells for women and children is to have a social service for abused women and children within the police system; a vehicle to access justice …. The programme will address the needs of the community of abused women and the police system. The differential strengths and contributions of the police system and the Special Cells enable a coordinated, multi-agency response to the issue of violence against women. Through its location in the police system, Special Cells create an emotional, physical, psychological, and legal space for the abused women within the criminal justice system, where they can address their needs and concerns within a facilitative environment.

The project is the demonstration of an ideology and a methodology, which has been effective in making the issue of violence against women visible, and in challenging violence itself. The expansion of the Special Cells project in Haryana should be seen in the light of the adverse girl child sex ratio, low status of women, and violence against them …. It becomes the duty of the state to provide a facility or service in response to violence against women, because the socio-economic and political environment of the country is changing rapidly and traditional family kinship ties are loosening. In this situation, the following structure and budget is suggested for the institutionalisation of Special Cells for women and children in Haryana state.

From Suggested Structure and Administration of the Special Cells

Every Special Cell needs to have a uniform structure and administration.

Each Special Cell has two trained social workers, who are full-time paid workers.

Each Special Cell is located in a police station or office.

Each Special Cell shares infrastructure with the police station or office where it is located.

The organisational development of Special Cells can be helped by partners from civil society or academic institutions.

A project coordinator and a state-level monitoring committee will jointly oversee the work of the Special Cells.

There will be regular interaction and sharing of ideas with the police, right from the police station to the office of the nodal officer in the state headquarters.

From Conclusion

Based on the above guidelines, the Special Cells offer rich possibilities for scaling up and replication, as the experiences in Maharashtra and Rajasthan indicate. Finally, while these ideas can provide guidance for strategic planning for institutionalising the Special Cells, there would be a need to evolve a mechanism/body that takes the responsibility to see to its smooth implementation, continued support and funding within the police system, and its structural relationship with the state. Drawing on the specific experiences of Maharashtra, where Special Cells have now become a state-sponsored government scheme (monitored by the Home Department and funded by the Department of Women and Child Development), and Rajasthan, where Special Cells are run by women's groups in partnership with the police, Haryana state can consider the structure for the institutionalisation of the Special Cells within context-specific requirements.

Appendix 6

A Sample Police Training Feedback Report

Millennium Vision Training Programme, Thane

Thirty-five participants evaluated this programme by filling out a questionnaire. The exercise was aimed at gauging the relevance of the programme. It also sought to evaluate its content and methodology, find out whether it was informative and thought provoking, and whether the subjects covered were adequate.

Relevance of the Topics Covered in the Training

Most participants felt that the subjects covered by the training programme were related to their daily work. It was generally perceived that the topics covered would benefit them in handling day-to-day cases involving women and children better. They felt that they would be able to deal with these cases more effectively, and communicate with women better. It was also felt that the training provided a better understanding of 'domestic violence', with the issues related to such violence spelt out more clearly. The group also drew insights into different types of violence against women.

Most of the participants felt that the topics covered were thought provoking. A couple of participants stated that after the training, they would be able to pay more attention to nuances and finer details during investigations into violence against women. These are at times overlooked now.

New Information Gained through the Training

The participants felt that the sharing of ideas had helped them to gain new information. On knowledge about violence against women, a couple of participants felt that they had received specific and relevant information on this, which had helped to reorient their attitude towards women.

Attitudinal Shifts and Reorientation

An attitudinal shift helped the participants to better understand the nature of the assistance required by a woman who comes to the police station. One participant recognised the necessity of paying attention to small details during investigation and while writing FIRs, especially in cases related to women and children. Another participant felt that the training had given him a new perspective.

Addressing Issues of Accountability and Collaboration with NGOs

The implications of the involvement of NGOs and the concomitant issue of accountability while working with the police system also came up, and were recognised during the evaluation. Two of the participants felt that they would not be able to coordinate with NGOs in their work.

Some participants felt that the programme would help in improving the image of the police in society. This would also help them in changing their attitude in cases of violence against women. They felt that they would be able to communicate better with women and children.

It was felt that there would be more coordination with women's organisations, and that this would help the police in investigation. Two participants opined that while the technical details of the cases were important, it was equally important to understand the sensibility of the abused woman, who had been through a traumatic time.

Significance of the Training

Regarding the extent to which the programme was found helpful to their work, 29 participants felt it was helpful, two participants did not find it so, and two did not respond.

It was felt that this programme would help the police in investigation. It was also felt that they had received more insight into the way judges thought, and the important points that should be considered during investigation. They also picked up tips on how to record FIRs and present chargesheets in court for effective prosecution.

They came to know about new amendments and laws, including the Protection of Women from Domestic Violence Bill. In addition, they realised that good communication with violated women was very important, and the significance of this was brought out in the training.

One of the public prosecutors said that he would now be able to help the police in effective investigation and work better with them.

The participants gained information on the Rape Kit, and on child sexual abuse. Eight participants felt that forensic investigation would be helpful.

One participant stated that he realised where he had lapsed in dealing with women, and that there would be a change in his attitude towards women.

Responses to the Methodology Used

Almost all participants liked the methodology used. One participant did not respond. Two of the participants felt that there was less interaction and discussion.

Some participants pointed to the need for more training material to be provided in future courses. Some also felt that there should be more visual presentations, especially on forensic investigation.

The public prosecutor felt that the details of the programme should be given in advance. Two of the participants felt there should be more question and answer sessions. Two others felt that more police officers and psychologists should be involved, and more case laws should be discussed.

There was also mention of including fingerprint experts, DNA experts, forensic experts, and legal experts. Some felt that there should be role playing to demonstrate effective communication. But the general view of the participants was that the topics covered were adequate.

Usefulness of the Programme in Daily Work

The participants felt that the programme would be helpful in their daily work. They also felt that they would be able to convey their knowledge on violence against women and child sexual abuse to their colleagues.

It was felt that the information on collecting samples for forensic investigation was very useful.

Almost all felt that the programme schedule, venue and resources were good. Two felt that the space was too small for group discussions, while another two felt that the programme should have been for 10–15 days.

References

Agarwal, B., 'Bargaining and Gender Relations: Within and Beyond the Household', *Feminist Economics* 3 (1), 1997, pp. 1–51.

Apte, V., 'Evaluation Study of the Special Cells', Internal Report, Mumbai: Tata Institute of Social Sciences (TISS), 2004.

The Boston Women's Health Collective, *The New Our Bodies Ourselves: A Book by and for Women*, New York: Touchstone, 1992.

Chakravarty, S., 'Mainstreaming Gender in the Police: The Maharashtra Experience', *Development in Practice* 8 (4), 1998, pp. 430–438.

Chatterjee, P., *The Nation and Its Fragments: Colonial and Postcolonial Histories,* Princeton, NJ: Princeton University Press, 1993.

Chikarmane, Poornima, 'Too Big for their Boots: Women and the Policing of Violence against Women', in N. Kabeer and R. Subrahmanian (eds), *Institutions, Relations and Outcomes*, New Delhi: Kali for Women, 1999.

Dave, A., 'Strategic Alliance, A Way Forward for Violence against Women: A Case for the Special Cells, India', *Violence against Women Journal,* September 2013.

Dave, A. and A. Dharmadhikari, 'Working with the Establishment: A New Challenge', *Indian Journal of Social Work* XLVIII (3), 1987.

Dave, A. and G. Solanki, 'Journey from Violence to Crime; A Study of Domestic Violence in the City of Mumbai,' Unpublished Research Report, Mumbai: Tata Institute of Social Sciences (TISS), 2000.

Dave, A., G. Solanki and P. Basu, 'An Ongoing Journey: Learning from a Field Action Project in the Police System', *Indian Journal of Social Work* 61 (April), 2000.

Desai, M., M. Pimple and S. Jaswal, 'Social Work Education and its Application to General University Education: An Interview with Professor Armaity Desai', *Indian Journal of Social Work* 61 (April), 2000.

Foucault, Michel, *Power/knowledge Selected Interviews and Other Writings 1972–1977*, Colin Gordon (ed.), New York: Pantheon Books, 1980.

————, *Discipline and Punish: The Birth of the Prison*, New York: Vintage, 1995.

Freire, Paulo, *Pedagogy of the Oppressed*, Harmondsworth, UK: Penguin, 1972.

Friedman, Lawrence J., *Identity's Architect: A Biography of Erik H. Erikson*, Cambridge, MA: Harvard University Press, 1999.

Gilligan, Carol, *In a Different Voice: Psychological Theory and Women's Development*, Cambridge, MA: Harvard University Press, 1982.

International Institute of Population Studies (IIPS), *National Family Health Survey (NFHS-3)*, Volume I, 2005–2006, New Delhi: Ministry of Health and Family Welfare, Government of India, pp. 498–519.

Jaswal, Surinder, *Examining Health Records for Evidence of Domestic Violence: A Research Study in Maharashtra, India*, Mumbai: Tata Institute of Social Sciences, 2000.

Kabeer, N., *Reversed Realities: Gender Hierarchies in Development Thought*, New Delhi: Kali for Women, 1995.

Mayoux, L., 'Micro-finance and the Empowerment of Women: A Review of Key Issues', SFP Working Paper No. 23, Geneva: International Labour Organization (ILO), 2000.

McElhinny, Bonnie S., 'Challenging Hegemonic Masculinities: Female and Male Police Officers Handling Domestic Violence', in K. Hall and M. Bucholtz (eds), *Gender Articulated: Language and the Socially Constructed Self*, New York: Routledge, 1995.

Mitra, Nishi, *Domestic Violence as a Public Issue: A Review of Responses*, Mumbai: Unit for Women Studies, Tata Institute of Social Sciences, 2000.

Nagraj, Vijay, 'The Politics of Disease: An Exploration into the High Incidence of Tuberculosis among Women Survivors and Domestic Violence', Unpublished Course Work, Mumbai: Tata Institute of Social Sciences, 1996.

Nussbaum, Martha C. and A. Sen (eds), *The Quality of Life*, Oxford: Clarendon Press, 1993.

Nussbaum, Martha C., *Women and Human Development: The Capabilities Approach*, Cambridge: Cambridge University Press, 2000.

Panchal, Trupti and Nahida Shaikh, 'Documentation of Police Cases of Sexually Abused Girls in Mumbai City between 1994 and 1995,' Special Cells, Tata Institute of Social Sciences, Mumbai, 1997.

Pearce, Diana, 'The Feminization of Poverty: Women, Work, and Welfare', *Urban and Social Change Review* 11, 1978, pp. 28–36.

Purvin, D., 'Weaving a Tangled Safety Net; The Intergenerational Legacy of Domestic Violence and Poverty', *Violence against Women Journal* 9 (10), 2003.

Resource Centre for Intervention on Violence against Women (RCIVAW-TISS), 'Case Study-cum-Report of Work from 2008–2012 in the Establishment and Institutionalisation of Special Cells for Women and Children in Haryana', Unpublished report, in collaboration with the Haryana Police and State Department of Women and Child Development, 2013.

Robeyns, Ingrid, 'Sen's Capability Approach and Gender Inequality: Selecting Relevant Capabilities', *Feminist Economics* 9 (2–3), 2003a, pp. 61–92.

————, 'Is Nancy Fraser's Critique of Theories of Distributive Justice Justified?' *Constellations* 10 (4), 2003b.

Rubin, G., 'The Traffic in Women: Notes on the Political Economy of Sex', in Linda Nicholson (ed.), *The Second Wave: Reader in Feminist Theory*, New York and London: Routledge, 1997.

Sen, A., *Development as Freedom*, Oxford: Oxford University Press, 2000.

Sen, A. and J. Dreze, *Hunger and Public Action*, Oxford: Oxford University Press, 1998.

Special Cell, 'Because the Personal is Political: Study of Special Cells Records', Unpublished Research Report, Tata Institute of Social Sciences, Mumbai, 1997.

————, 'Shades of Courage; Women and IPC Section 498A', Unpublished Report, Tata Institute of Social Sciences, Mumbai, 1999.

————, 'TISS: Special Cell for Women and Children within the Maharashtra State Police System', in Renuka Mishra (ed.), *Compendium on Good Practices in Police: Gender Issues*, Vol. IV, Hyderabad: Sardar Vallabhbhai Patel National Police Academy, 2004.

————, 'Report on Training of Trainers on Violence against Women for Police Officers in Orissa', Internal Document, Tata Institute of Social Sciences, Mumbai, 2008.

————, 'Report of the Training Programme on Violence against Women and Helping Skills for Police Personnel, Delhi', Internal Document, Tata Institute of Social Sciences, Mumbai, 2009.

Stark, Evan, *Coercive Control: The Entrapment of Women in Personal Life*, New York: Oxford University Press, 2007

Walby, Sylvia, *Theorizing Patriarchy*, Cambridge, MA: Basil Blackwell, 1990.

Wyatt, Robin, *Broken Mirrors: The 'Dowry Problem' in India*, New Delhi: Sage Publications, 2011.

About the Author

Anjali Dave is Professor, Centre for Equity for Women, Children and Families, School of Social Work, Tata Institute of Social Sciences, Mumbai. She has engaged in two vital areas/processes—developing socio-legal interventions and research on violence against women; and developing critical and effective trained social work personnel for social justice. She has been a member of several national- and state-level government committees for policy on women's issues, gender trainings, and on Violence against Women.